SO YOU *think* YOU KNOW Taylor Swift?

PROVE IT!

PENGUIN BOOKS

UK | USA | Canada | Ireland | Australia
India | New Zealand | South Africa | China

Penguin Random House Australia is part of the Penguin Random House group of companies whose addresses can be found at global.penguinrandomhouse.com.

First published by Penguin Books, an imprint of Penguin Random House Australia Pty Ltd, in 2024

Cover design by Caroline Lee © Penguin Random House Australia Pty Ltd
Internal design by Julie Hally
Internal illustrations by Melissa Lane
Cover image used under license from Shutterstock.com

Printed and bound in Australia by Griffin Press, an accredited ISO AS/NZS 14001 Environmental Management Systems printer

A catalogue record for this book is available from the National Library of Australia

ISBN 978 1 76 135242 3 (Paperback)

Penguin Random House Australia uses papers that are natural and recyclable products, made from wood grown in sustainable forests. The logging and manufacture processes are expected to conform to the environmental regulations of the country of origin.

penguin.com.au

We at Penguin Random House Australia acknowledge that Aboriginal and Torres Strait Islander peoples are the Traditional Custodians and the first storytellers of the lands on which we live and work. We honour Aboriginal and Torres Strait Islander peoples' continuous connection to Country, waters, skies and communities. We celebrate Aboriginal and Torres Strait Islander stories, traditions and living cultures; and we pay our respects to Elders past and present.

CONTENTS

LEVEL 1 – LET THE GAMES BEGIN 1

LEVEL 2 – FILLING IN THE BLANKS AS YOU GO 17

LEVEL 3 – THESE FACTS ARE NOTHING NEW 35

LEVEL 4 – YOU DON'T HAVE TO ANSWER JUST 'CAUSE WE ASKED YOU (BUT YOU SHOULD) 53

LEVEL 5 – BRING ON THE PRETENDERS, YOU'RE NOT AFRAID 71

LEVEL 6 – IT'S GETTING DIFFICULT BUT IT'S REAL 89

LEVEL 7 – WHO ELSE KNOWS TAYLOR LIKE YOU? NOBODY. 107

MONDEGREENS 124

LEVEL 8 – THESE LINGERING QUESTIONS KEEP YOU UP 127

LEVEL 9 – YOU CAN BUILD A CASTLE OUT OF ALL THE THINGS YOU KNOW ABOUT TAYLOR SWIFT 145

LEVEL 10 – I BET YOU THINK ABOUT TAYLOR SWIFT (A LOT) 163

LEVEL 11 – YOU ARE DEFINED BY THE THING YOU LOVE (TAYLOR SWIFT) 181

LEVEL 12 – YOU KNOW TAYLOR LIKE THE BACK OF YOUR HAND 199

LEVEL 13 – YOU ARE A MASTERMIND 217

ANSWERS 234

Being a Swiftie can be serious business.
Or not. You decide!

Jump around the pages of questions and activities to find what interests you – lyrics, album releases, relationships and awards, OR:

Answer all the questions in order and keep track of your score on each level as they get harder and harder.

Take a break by deciphering the friendship bracelets, laughing at mondegreens and solving find-a-words.

All of the answers are at the back. When you look at them is up to you and your conscience.

This book could be the perfect way to prove your fan status once and for all!

How much do you **THINK** you **KNOW** about the Chairman of our Tortured Poets Department?

Grab your fountain pen, glitter gel pen or quill to fill in the blank spaces yourself.

Grab your friends to fill it out together. Are you competitive? You can play against each other or form a team!

LEVEL 1

LET THE GAMES BEGIN

1. What is Taylor's middle name?

A. ____________________

2. What is Taylor's lucky number?

√ OR ✗

A. ____________________

3. What is Taylor's date of birth?

√ OR ✗

A. ____________________

4. What is Taylor's mother's name?

A. 

5. What is Taylor's father's name?

√ OR ✗

A. ______________________________

6. What is Taylor's brother's name?

√ OR ✗

A. ______________________________

7. Where was Taylor born?

√ OR ✗

A. ______________________________

8. What is Taylor's star sign?

√ OR ✗

A. ______________________________

9. What kind of farm did Taylor grow up on?

√ OR X

10. What are the names of Taylor's cats?

√ OR X

A. ____________________

11. Which music artist is Taylor named after?

√ OR X

A. ____________________

12. What is the name of Taylor's 2020 Netflix documentary?

✓ OR ✗

A. ____________________

13. What does *TV* refer to in terms of Taylor's album titles?

✓ OR ✗

A. ____________________

14. Finish this lyric from 'Shake It Off', 1989 (TV): 'It's like I got this ________ in my ________ saying it's gonna be ________'

✓ OR ✗

15. How old was Taylor when she signed her first record deal?

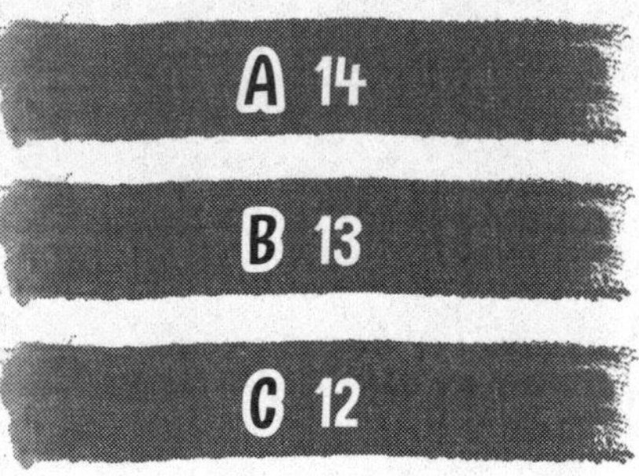

16. Which music artist famously interrupted Taylor's 2009 acceptance of an MTV Video Music Award for Best Female Video?

A. ____________________

17. What is Taylor's signature lipstick colour?

A. ____________________

18. What is the 'sister album' to *folklore*?

√ OR X

A. ______________________________

19. In 'Shake It Off', what is Taylor lightning on?

√ OR X

A. ______________________________

20. Which movie adaptation of a famed Broadway musical did Taylor have a role in?

√ OR X

A. ______________________________

21. Which album contains the song 'Delicate'?

√ OR X

A. ______________________________

22. What kind of jewellery have fans been known to wear to the Eras Tour?

A. ______________________

23. Which 'Down Bad' lyric is correct?

A 'NOW I'M DOWN BAD, CRYING IN THE GYM'

B 'NOW I'M DOWN BAD, CRYING AT THE GYM'

24. Taylor often inserts secret clues and messages in her music and videos for her fans. What are these called?

A. ______________________

25. Which song mentions a scarf left at an ex-boyfriend's sister's house?

A. ______________________________

26. Which 2020 album was Taylor's first 'alternative' album, a surprise release recorded during the COVID-19 pandemic?

A. ______________________________

27. Finish this lyric from 'Cruel Summer', *Lover*: 'Devils roll the dice,

________ ________,
________ ________'

28. Which album features the song 'Getaway Car'?

Ⓐ 1989 (TV)

Ⓑ REPUTATION

Ⓒ THE TORTURED POETS DEPARTMENT

29. What is the name of Taylor's second studio album?

✓ OR ✗

30. Finish this lyric from 'You Belong With Me', *Fearless (TV)*: 'She's cheer __________, and I'm on the __________'

✓ OR ✗

√ OR X

31. Which 'King of My Heart' lyric is correct?

A 'SALUTE TO ME, AS YOUR AMERICAN QUEEN'

B 'SALUTE TO ME, I'M YOUR AMERICAN QUEEN'

TRUE OR FALSE?

√ OR X

32. Taylor won her first Grammy Award for her album *Fearless*.

A. ______________________

33. Which 'The Best Day' lyric is correct?

√ OR X

A 'YOU SET UP A PAINT SET IN THE KITCHEN'

B 'YOU SET UP A PAINT BOX IN THE KITCHEN'

34. In which video does Taylor dress up as a man?

√ OR X

A. ______________________________

35. Finish this lyric from 'The Alchemy', *TTPD*: 'These ________ warm the ________, we been on a ________ ________'

√ OR X

36. Which city with bright lights does Taylor sing about on her *1989 (TV)* album?

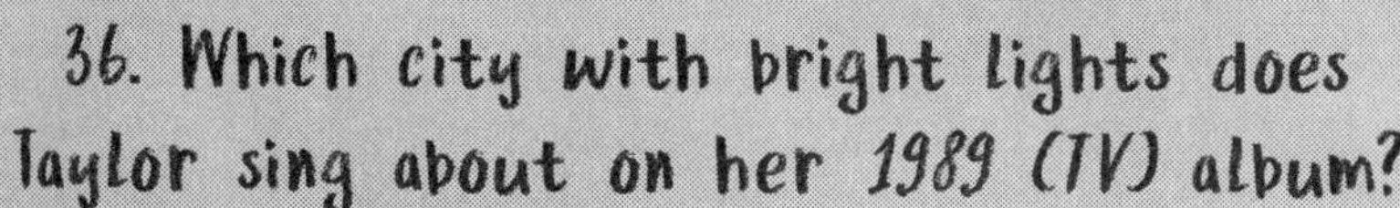

√ OR X

A. ______________________________

37. Which song references a wine-stained dress?

√ OR X

A. ______________________________

✓ OR ✗

38. Finish this lyric from 'Anti-Hero', Midnights: 'I'll stare directly at ________ ________ but never in ________ ________'

✓ OR ✗

39. Which album contains the song 'Our Song'?

A. ________________________________

✓ OR ✗

40. Which 'champagne problems' lyric is correct?

A 'YOUR MOM'S RING IN YOUR POCKET, MY PICTURE IN YOUR WALLET'

B 'YOUR MOM'S RING IN YOUR POCKET, MY PHOTO IN YOUR WALLET'

BAD BLOOD

J L E N A D U N H A M W E L V I N D A G R E A T R

C F C N N P Q P S E R A Y A H H X F M U L P M A J

M X O Y S E C V U Z K V K I T M G O Q J U T X R N

E Q U T V H O M E S L I C E L E I O N K N H F S X

N X P I K W R J Z N K O Y T W S G D U E A A M Y H

L T K A R L I E K L O S S E K J I E S N D I A N O

I U Z C I N D Y C R A W F O R D H S V D X L R J M

L C C V S S E L E N A G O M E Z A T X R A E I T E

Y A M K T M O A I H X G U U A Q D R Z I K E S H S

A R A X Y H O W M C E X P Q Q C I U E C X S K E S

L A D X C F E T V Q J A D P F C D C N K B T A T I

D D L K H E I C H U C E D I X X N T D L A E H R C

R E O N E A I O R E Q A S M S M C A A A D I A I E

I L V J I L Y U R I R L T S I A X X Y M B N R N L

D E E U T D L L F I M C M A I S F L A A L F G I L

G V M S C O F E E W S S H L S C T N R R O E I T I

E I A T C M R F N Y J Z O U L T A R I K O L T Y E

K N R I U I O E N P W X H N C L R A E Q D D A U G

N G T C T N S W G W O I D V C K V O L S V Q Y Z O

O N H E T O T T M D U M L L I U E G P B S G N G U

C E A B H D B R G A E Q P L O N R R X H A P A S L

K B H I R Q Y Y P Y G Z K E I R C S F X E I R L D

O J U K O Z T D I L E M M A O A Y D E U K X X A I

U Y N Q A Y E L Z Z A V C X I A M F I R C R D Y N

T V T I T K F Y N L N D V G C O S S H X D S J Z G

HAILEE STEINFELD
MARISKA HARGITAY
HAYLEY WILLIAMS
KENDRICK LAMAR
CARA DELEVINGNE
ELLIE GOULDING
CINDY CRAWFORD
LILY ALDRIDGE
SELENA GOMEZ
ELLEN POMPEO

JESSICA ALBA
KARLIE KLOSS
MARTHA HUNT
LENA DUNHAM
GIGI HADID
ZENDAYA
SERAYAH
BAD BLOOD
MAD LOVE
LUNA

KNOCKOUT
JUSTICE
ARSYN
DILEMMA
SLAY Z
DESTRUCTA X
CUT-THROAT
THE TRINITY
HOMESLICE

CATASTROPHE
LUCKY FIORI
MOTHER CHUCKER
HEADMISTRESS
WELVIN DA GREAT
THE CRIMSON CURSE
FROSTBYTE
DOMINO

YOU SCORED

__ __ /40!

Moving on is easy
for you to do . . .

LEVEL 2

FILLING IN THE BLANKS AS YOU GO

1. Which label did Taylor sign with for the release of her first six albums?

A. ____________________

TRUE OR FALSE?

2. Taylor is the only artist (as at 2024) to win Album of the Year at the Grammy Awards four times.

A. ____________________

3. What kind of car does Taylor sing about on *reputation*?

A. ____________________

4. What item of clothing does Taylor give away during the song '22' in the Eras Tour?

√ OR X

A. ______________________________

√ OR X

5. Finish this lyric from 'All You Had To Do Was Stay', 1989 (TV): 'Let me remind you, __________ __________, __________ __________ __________'

√ OR X

6. Which music artist features on 'Fortnight'?

A. ______________________________

7. What number is written on Taylor's hand in the 'I Can See You' music video?

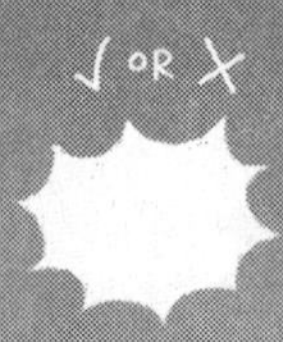

A. ______

8. Who directed Taylor in the music video for 'The Man'?

A. ______

9. Which album contains the song 'mad woman'?

A. ______

10. Which album title is lit up in neon in the music video for 'ME!'?

√ OR X

A. ____________________

11. Finish this lyric from 'The Prophecy', *TTPD*: 'Thought I caught ________ in a bottle'

√ OR X

12. Which album mentions the Cheshire Cat from *Alice's Adventures in Wonderland*?

√ OR X

A. ____________________

TRUE OR FALSE?

13. At age 11, Taylor sang the US national anthem for the Philadelphia 76ers.

A. ______________________________

14. Which two poets are mentioned in 'The Tortured Poets Department'?

A. ______________________________

15. For which song did Taylor win her first Grammy Award?

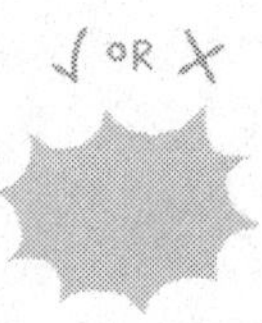

A. ______________________________

16. Who are the songs 'We Are Never Ever Getting Back Together' and 'All Too Well' allegedly about?

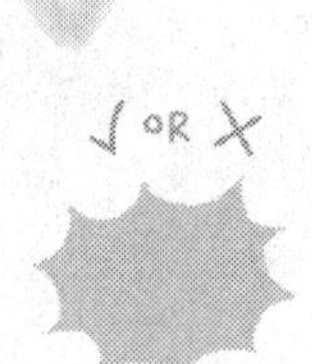

Ⓐ JOHN MAYER

Ⓑ JAKE GYLLENHAAL

Ⓒ TOM HIDDLESTON

17. In what renowned Nashville music venue was Taylor discovered?

A. ______________________________

18. What is the name of Taylor's management company?

A. ______________________________

19. Finish this lyric from 'Love Story', *Fearless (TV)*: "Cause you were Romeo, I was a ________ ________'

20. What is the name of Taylor's childhood best friend?

A. ____________________

21. Which of these songs is not on Taylor's debut album?

C 'OURS'

TRUE OR FALSE?

✓ OR ✗

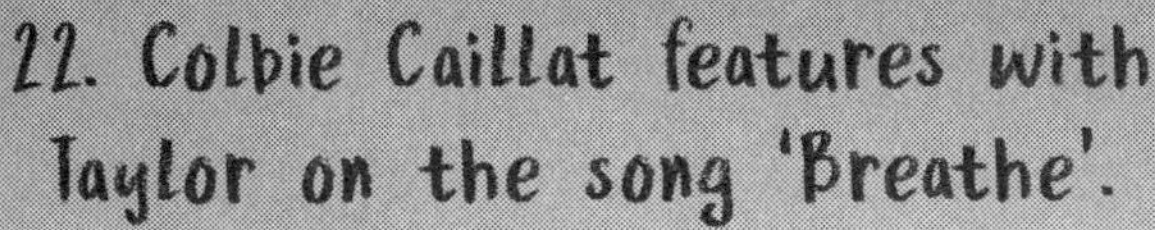

✓ OR ✗

23. Which album features the song 'Sad Beautiful Tragic'?

✓ OR ✗

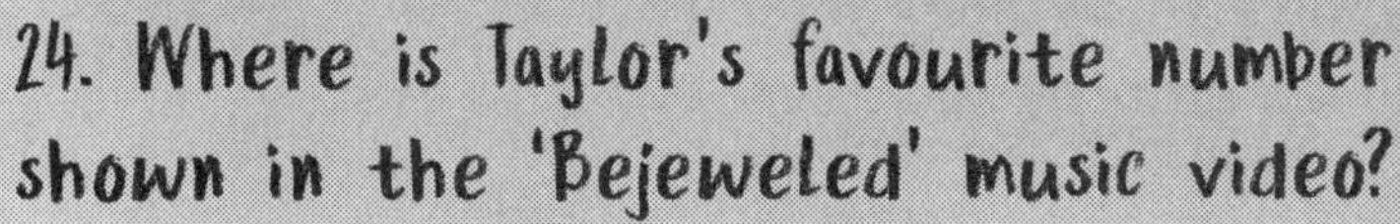

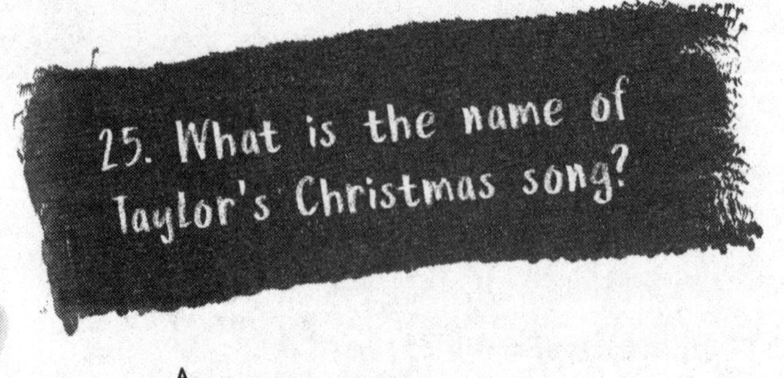

A. ______________________________

✓ OR ✗

26. Which 'Say Don't Go' lyric is correct?

A 'NOW YOUR SILENCE GOT ME SCREAMIN''

B 'NOW YOUR SILENCE HAS ME SCREAMIN''

27. Which album contains the song 'Mary's Song'?

A. ______________________________

✓ OR ✗

28. Finish this lyric from 'Dear John', *Speak Now (TV)*: 'The girl in the ________ cried the whole way home'

✓ OR ✗

29. Which Taylor album name is also a colour?

A. ________________________

✓ OR ✗

30. What is the name of the London bar featured on a song of the same name on *TTPD*?

A. ________________________

31. Finish this lyric from 'You're On Your Own, Kid', Midnights: 'I search the ________ of ________ ________'

√ OR X

32. Which Taylor album features 'Style' and 'Out Of The Woods'?

√ OR X

A. ________________________

33. Which album did Taylor call her first 'official pop album'?

√ OR X

A. ________________________

34. In which year did Taylor release her debut single 'Tim McGraw'?

A. ___________________________

35. Which 'the last great american dynasty' lyric is correct?

A 'AND BLEW THROUGH THE MONEY ON THE BOYS AND THE VALETS'

B 'AND BLEW THROUGH THE MONEY ON THE BOYS AND THE BALLET'

36. In which city did Taylor grow up before moving to Nashville?

A. ______________________________

TRUE OR FALSE?

37. Taylor wrote *Speak Now* entirely by herself.

A. ______________________________

38. What is the name of the male character Taylor sings about in 'betty'?

A. ______________________________

39. What item of clothing is also the name of a song on *folklore*?

A. ____________________

40. Which of the following songs is not on the *Red (TV)* album?

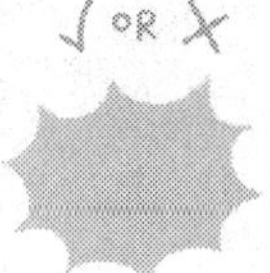

A 'BETTER MAN'

B 'I DO'

C 'BEGIN AGAIN'

DECODE THE FRIENDSHIP BRACELETS

A. ______________________________

____

A. ______________________________

____

A. ______________________________

____

YOU SCORED

___/40!

Moving on is easy
for you to do . . .

LEVEL 3

THESE FACTS ARE NOTHING NEW

1. Which song compares a famous Greek philosopher with a sportsman?

√ OR ✗

Ⓐ 'THE ARCHER'

Ⓑ 'SO HIGH SCHOOL'

Ⓒ 'EVERYTHING HAS CHANGED'

TRUE OR FALSE?

2. Taylor was 11 when she wrote her first song.

√ OR ✗

A. ______________________________

3. Who is 'Back to December' rumoured to be about?

✓ OR ✗

A. ______________________

4. What costumes did Taylor and Katy Perry wear when they appeared together in the 'You Need To Calm Down' music video?

✓ OR ✗

TAYLOR: ______________________

KATY: ______________________

5. What kind of stage does Taylor not like in 'Look What You Made Me Do'?

✓ OR ✗

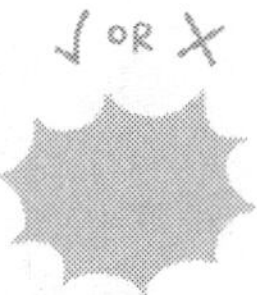

A. ______________________

6. Which two actors did Taylor feature in her 'All Too Well' music video/short film?

✓ OR ✗

A. ______________________________

____

7. Finish this lyric from 'Gorgeous', reputation: 'If you've got a ________, I'm ________, ________ ________'

✓ OR ✗

8. Which band members play the evil stepsisters in the 'Bejeweled' music video?

✓ OR ✗

A. ______________________________

9. Finish this lyric from 'loml', *TTPD*: 'If you know it in one ________, it's ________'

√ OR X

10. Which song references plaid shirt days?

A. ________________

√ OR X

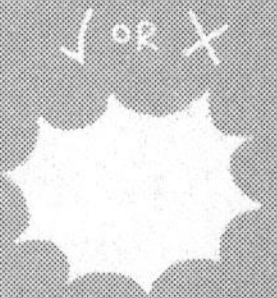

11. What was the name of Taylor's first concert tour?

A. ________________

12. Which of Taylor's exes is the topic of many songs on the Lover album?

A. ____________________

13. What was Taylor's training regime in the lead-up to the Eras Tour?

A. ____________________

TRUE OR FALSE?

14. Taylor was 19 when she won her first Grammy Award.

A. ____________________

15. Who is the song 'Bad Blood' rumoured to be about?

A KIM KARDASHIAN

B KATY PERRY

C KHLOE KARDASHIAN

16. Which lyric to 'Karma' did Taylor change on the Eras Tour?

A. ____

17. Which American holiday did Taylor throw famous parties to celebrate?

A. ____

TRUE OR FALSE?

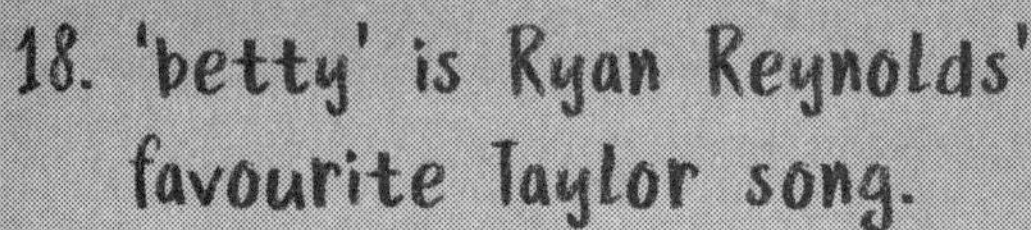

18. 'betty' is Ryan Reynolds' favourite Taylor song.

✓ OR ✗

A. ______________________

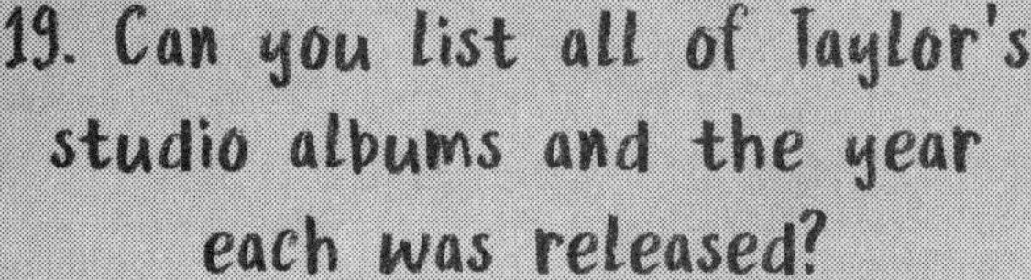

19. Can you list all of Taylor's studio albums and the year each was released?

✓ OR ✗

A. ______________________

√ OR X

20. Which 'You're On Your Own, Kid' lyric is correct?

A 'I TOUCH MY PHONE LIKE IT'S YOUR FACE'

B 'I TOUCH MY PHONE AS IF IT'S YOUR FACE'

√ OR X

21. Which music artist features on the song 'ME!'?

A. ______________________________

√ OR X

22. What was the lead single on Taylor's debut album?

A. ______________________________

23. Which of these songs appears on the 3am edition of *Midnights*?

√ OR X

A 'LABYRINTH'

B 'KARMA'

C 'DEAR READER'

√ OR X

24. Finish this lyric from 'Bad Blood', *1989 (TV)*: 'You know it used to be ________ ________, so take a ________ what you've ________'

25. How did Taylor sign off her endorsement of Kamala Harris in the 2024 US election?

√ OR X

A. ____________________

26. How many studio albums has Taylor released as at July 2024?

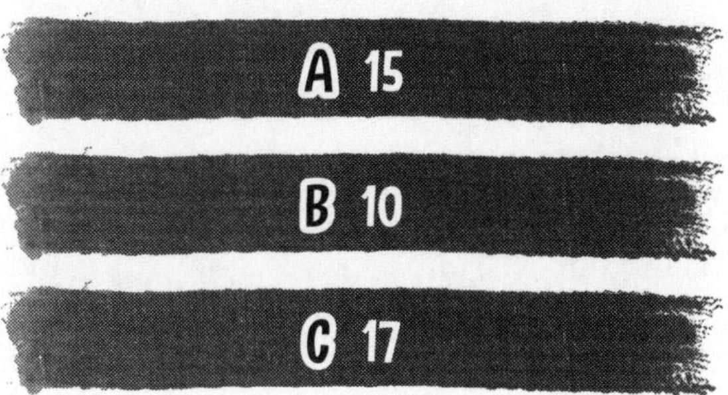

27. Which song from *Midnights* mentions friendship bracelets?

A. ______________________________

28. Finish this lyric from *evermore*:
'She'll patch up your ________
that I shred'

29. Which two seasons are referenced in 'Forever Winter'?

A. ______________________________

30. Which late, iconic actor is named in 'Style'?

✓ OR ✗

A. ______________________________

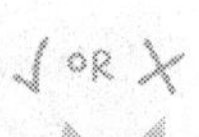

31. Who, according to Taylor, is the problem in 'Anti-Hero'?

A. ______________________________

32. How did Taylor refer to 'betty', 'cardigan' and 'august'?

✓ OR ✗

A. ______

33. Which boy does Taylor sing about in 'Teardrops On My Guitar'?

✓ OR ✗

A. ______

34. What is the name of the song Taylor wrote about her experience with bullying?

✓ OR ✗

A. ______

35. What controversial lyric did Taylor change in 'Picture to Burn'?

A. ______________________

36. Which song opens with the lyric: 'I stay out too late'?

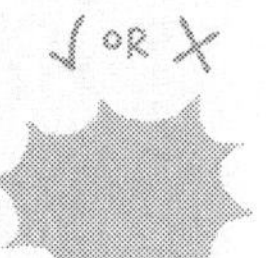

A. ______________________

37. Which album includes the tracks 'Haunted' and 'Innocent'?

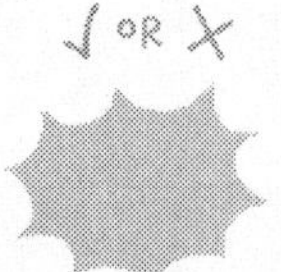

A. ______________________

38. What month is also the name of a song on *folklore*?

A. ______________________________

39. Which lyric from 'Hits Different' is correct?

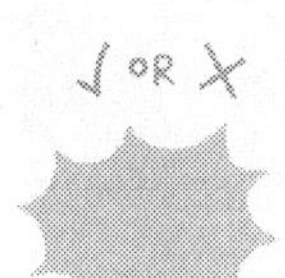

A 'I USED TO SWITCH OUT THESE KENS, I'D JUST GHOST'

B 'I USED TO SWITCH OUT THESE KENS, I'D JUST GO'

40. What time was Taylor's watch choker set to at the 2024 Grammy awards?

A. ______________________________

```
S S H N C P N Q J A I P Z W X D V M A V V X R Y E
E M M A S T O N E L H R Q V M B E M S I S Y C I L
M H G N T L I L Y A L D R I D G E D K Y W G Y C O
X Q A S Q H U C U Y M A J R F O N W L X G K L E R
E A B I S H A D G R H A Y L E Y W I L L I A M S D
A Q I E L N C O N X J X T D N Z C G D D B K C P E
S R G G L E L E N A D U N H A M T Q A A F J R I Y
A Q A K A C E U R U A F J U V D C Z N T S A U C O
B O I W U N J S Z Z R P N Y Z A S M I S A F P E G
R A L B R C B K T H J I A I W N Z A E A D C Q L I
I V A Z A F N C G E U A A S W M T O L L I A Q A G
N R N O D I H M J U I B I Z K X M H L Z E R C L I
A I D E E B R I T T A N Y M A H O M E S S A A A H
C L E K R A K R Q S Z A F T E W L N H W I D M N A
A L R R N L A N A D E L R E Y K W H A U N E I A D
R A S A L E S T E H A I M T L S I S I F K L L H I
P V O V D O U L I L N K G M L D O N M U E E A A D
E I N I K B S O P H I E T U R N E R G K W V C I M
N G A T S V D Y I V T E D H A Z O N Z O V I A M W
T N L Z E L L I E G O U L D I N G L Y W L N B B D
E E P B B C F F E N K P H O E B E B R I D G E R S
R G G W L S U K I W A T E R H O U S E Z L N L F H
C R S F B S L S S E L E N A G O M E Z E Q E L H L
T F B L A K E L I V E L Y G F D I B I H G H O O S
D I A R F R A P F M L K E L E I G H T E L L E R G
```

SABRINA CARPENTER
ABIGAIL ANDERSON
HAILEE STEINFELD
CARA DELEVINGNE
BRITTANY MAHOMES
HAYLEY WILLIAMS
PHOEBE BRIDGERS
SUKI WATERHOUSE
ELLIE GOULDING
CAMILA CABELLO
KELEIGH TELLER
LILY ALDRIDGE
DANIELLE HAIM
SOPHIE TURNER
AVRIL LAVIGNE
BLAKE LIVELY
LENA DUNHAM
LANA DEL REY
EMMA STONE
ALANA HAIM
SELENA GOMEZ
JAIME KING
ESTE HAIM
ZOË KRAVITZ
LAURA DERN
SADIE SINK
GIGI HADID
ICE SPICE
LORDE

YOU SCORED
___/40!

Moving on is easy
for you to do . . .

LEVEL 4

YOU DON'T HAVE TO ANSWER JUST 'CAUSE WE ASKED YOU

(BUT YOU SHOULD)

1. Which of Taylor's exes has appeared on stage during her Eras Tour?

√ OR X

A. ____________________

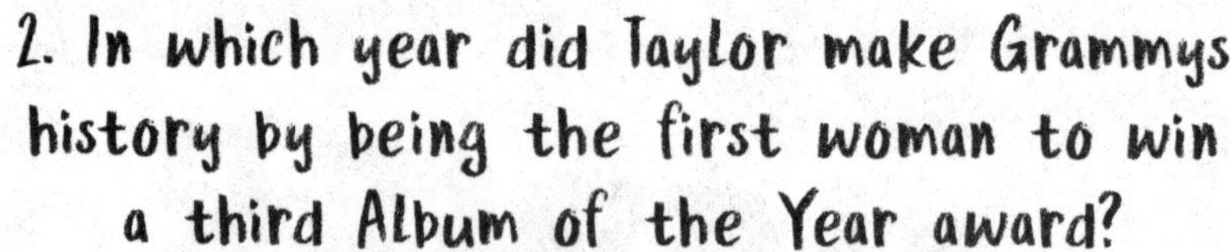

2. In which year did Taylor make Grammys history by being the first woman to win a third Album of the Year award?

√ OR X

Ⓐ 2022

Ⓑ 2024

Ⓒ 2021

√ OR X

3. Which song did Taylor write for the film *Valentine's Day*?

A. ____________________

TRUE OR FALSE?

✓ OR ✗

4. The following celebrities all appear in the 'You Need To Calm Down' music video: Katy Perry, Adam Lambert, Ellen DeGeneres, Ryan Reynolds, RuPaul, Billy Porter, Todrick Hall, Laverne Cox, Chester Lockhart, Tan France, Antoni Porowski, Karamo Brown, Jonathan Van Ness, Bobby Berk, Ciara, Jesse Tyler Ferguson, Hayley Kiyoko, Adam Rippon, Hannah Hart, Dexter Mayfield.

A. ______________________________

✓ OR ✗

5. Which music artist features on 'Florida!!!'?

A. ______________________________

✓ OR ✗

6. What kind of dreams does Taylor sing about on *1989 (TV)*?

A. ______________________________

✓ OR ✗

7. What connection does Taylor have to famed heiress Rebekah Harkness?

A. ______________________________

✓ OR ✗

8. In which 2012 animated film did Taylor play a voice role?

A. ______________________________

9. Finish this lyric from 'ME!', Lover: 'You can't spell "awesome" without ________'

✓ OR ✗

10. In which song at the Eras Tour does the crowd chant, 'You forgive, you forget, but you never let it go,' to Taylor?

✓ OR ✗

A. ____________________

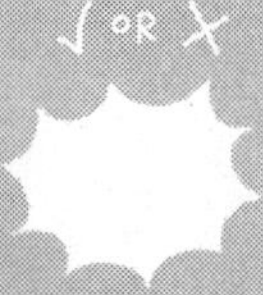

11. What category did Taylor win when Kanye West interrupted her MTV Video Music Award acceptance speech?

✓ OR ✗

A. ____________________

12. Which late basketballer's daughter did Taylor gift her hat to in Los Angeles on the Eras Tour?

A. ______________________________

13. Which label is Taylor signed to now?

A. ______________________________

14. Finish this lyric from 'Dear John', Speak Now (TV): 'You paint me a ________ ________, then go back and turn it to ________.'

15. What is Travis Kelce's jersey number?

√ OR X

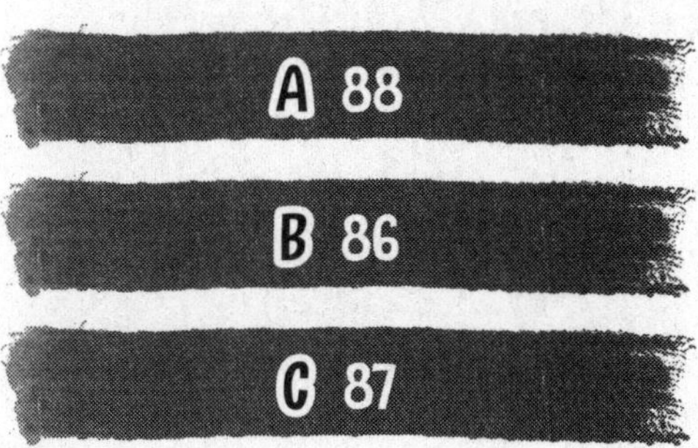

16. Which of Taylor's exes is reportedly the topic of many songs on the *1989 (TV)* album?

√ OR X

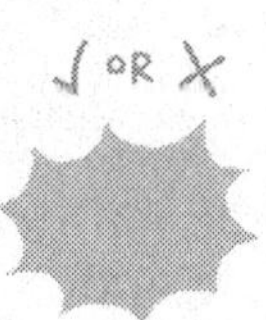

A. ______________________________

17. Which 'All Too Well' lyric is correct?

A 'BUT MAYBE THIS THING WAS A MASTERPIECE TILL YOU TORE IT ALL UP'

√ OR X

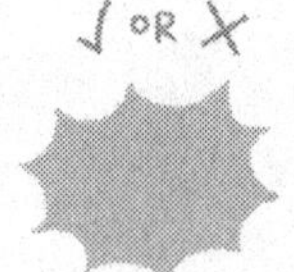

B 'BUT MAYBE THIS THING WAS A MASTERPIECE TILL YOU RIPPED IT ALL UP'

18. Which two songs did Taylor write for *The Hunger Games* soundtrack?

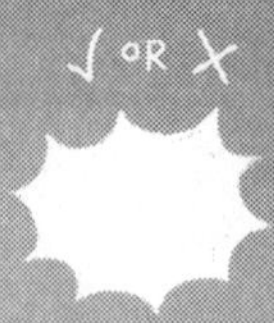

A. ____________________

19. Finish this lyric from 'thanK you aIMee', TTPD: 'There wouldn't be ________, if there hadn't been ________'

✓ OR ✗

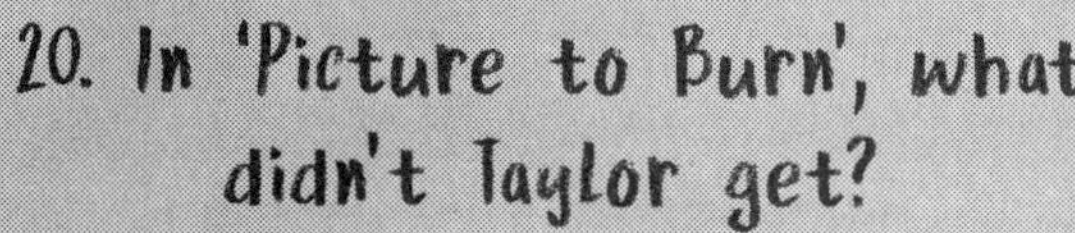

20. In 'Picture to Burn', what didn't Taylor get?

✓ OR ✗

A. ____________________

21. What year was the single 'Bad Blood' released?

√ OR X

A. ______________________________

22. What European city does Taylor sing about on *Midnights* (3am Edition)?

√ OR X

A. ______________________________

23. Finish this lyric from 'loml', *TTPD*: 'What we thought ________ ________ ________, time was ________

√ OR X

24. What colour dress is referenced in 'Is It Over Now?'?

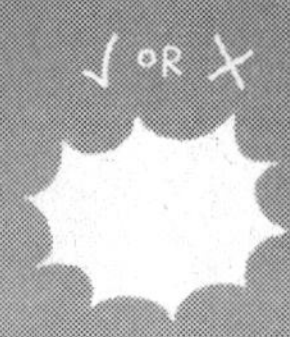

A BLUE

B RED

C BLACK

25. What item does RuPaul present in the 'You Need To Calm Down' music video?

A. ______________________

26. What was the album *Lover* originally going to be called?

A. ______________________

27. In which song does Taylor mention herself by her full name?

A. ______________________________

28. Which 'The Alchemy' lyric is correct?

A 'CALL THE AMATEURS AND CULL 'EM FROM THE TEAM'

B 'CALL THE AMATEURS AND CUT 'EM FROM THE TEAM'

29. Which song mentions the main character dyeing a dog key-lime green?

A. ______________________________

30. Which band performs on 'coney island' on *evermore*?

A. ______________________________

31. Finish this lyric from 'this is me trying', *folklore*: 'They told me all of my ________ were ________'

32. Which New York City street is the name of a song on *Lover*?

A. ______________________________

33. Which artists feature on The Vault songs on *Speak Now (TV)*?

A. ______

34. 'We Are Never Ever Getting Back Together' was co-written with which famous producers?

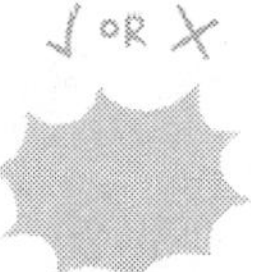

A. ______

35. Which song did Taylor write for the *Fifty Shades Darker* soundtrack?

A. ______

36. Which song begins with: 'Say you're sorry'?

√ or X

A. ____________________

37. Which of Taylor's albums ends with 'Begin Again'?

√ or X

A. ____________________

√ or X

38. What day and date did Taylor turn 13?

A. ____________________

39. Which album contains the track 'New Romantics'?

A. ______________________________

40. What iconic landmark is seen in the background as Selena Gomez kicks Taylor out the window in the opening of the 'Bad Blood' music video?

A THE EMPIRE STATE BUILDING, NYC

B TOWER BRIDGE, LONDON

C THE OPERA HOUSE, SYDNEY

DECODE THE FRIENDSHIP BRACELETS

YOU SCORED ___/40!

Moving on is easy for you to do . . .

LEVEL 5

BRING ON THE PRETENDERS, YOU'RE NOT AFRAID

TRUE OR FALSE?

1. In the 'Anti-Hero' music video, Taylor's three cats are listed as the beneficiaries of her will.

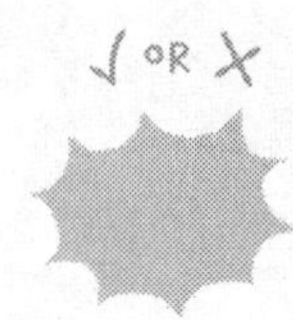

A. ________________________

2. Which 'Fortnight' lyric is correct?

A 'I TOOK THE MIRACLE MOVE-ON DRUG, THE EFFECTS WERE TEMPORARY'

B 'I TOOK A MIRACLE MOVE-ON DRUG, THE EFFECTS WERE TEMPORARY'

3. What is written on the first tombstone shown in the 'Look What You Made Me Do' music video?

√ OR X

A. ______________________________

4. Which song starts with: 'You should've been there'?

√ OR X

A. ______________________________

5. Finish this lyric from 'Fifteen', *Fearless (TV)*: 'You sit in class next to a ________, ________ ________'

√ OR X

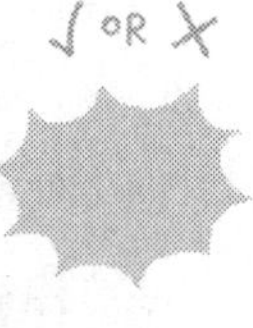

6. Which music video depicts Taylor as a film star?

A. ____________________

7. Which 'Hey Stephen' lyric is correct?

✓ OR ✗

A 'THE WAY YOU TALK, WAY YOU WALK, WAY YOU SAY MY NAME'

B 'THE WAY YOU WALK, WAY YOU TALK, WAY YOU SAY MY NAME'

8. What was printed on a T-shirt famously worn by Tom Hiddleston at Taylor's 4th July party in 2016?

A. ____________________

9. Which song did Taylor change the lyrics to live on stage to reference her new relationship with Travis Kelce on the Eras Tour?

A. ____________________

10. Taylor allegedly wrote 'Forever & Always' and 'Mr Perfectly Fine' about which Jonas brother?

✓ OR ✗

A JOE

B KEVIN

C NICK

11. What hangs on the wall inside the vault Taylor is trapped in, in the 'I Can See You' music video?

A. ____________________

12. Which of the following films is one of Taylor's favourites?

√ OR X

Ⓐ SPY KIDS

Ⓑ TITANIC

Ⓒ LOVE ACTUALLY

13. What is the name of the Christmas Tree farm Taylor grew up on?

√ OR X

A. ______________________________

TRUE OR FALSE?

14. Taylor's maternal grandmother, Marjorie, can be heard singing on the song 'Marjorie'.

√ OR X

A. ______________________________

15. Which album features a collaboration with The Chicks?

A. ______________________________

16. Who is the song 'The Best Day' about?

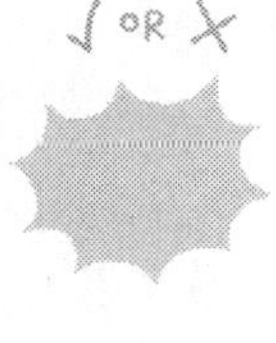

A TAYLOR'S DAD

B TAYLOR'S MUM

C TAYLOR'S CATS

√ OR X

17. Finish this lyric from 'All You Had To Do Was Stay', *1989 (TV)*: 'The more I think about it now, ________ ________ ________ ________ '

18. Which song did Taylor perform at the 2009 MTV Video Music Awards, leading to the infamous Kanye West interruption?

A. ______________________________

TRUE OR FALSE?

19. 'End Game' features Ed Sheeran and Snoop Dogg.

A. ______________________________

20. Christian Louboutin designed which part of Taylor's outfits for the European leg of the Eras Tour?

A. ______________________________

21. With which singer/songwriter did Taylor re-record 'Lover' as a duet?

√ OR ✗

A. ____________________

22. Finish this lyric from 'loml', TTPD: 'Who's gonna stop us from ________ back into ________ ________.'

√ OR ✗

23. Which album contains the song 'Tied Together with a Smile'?

√ OR ✗

A. ____________________

24. Which songs from *folklore* and *TTPD* reference a classic Lewis Carroll story?

A. ____________________

25. Which of the following songs is not on the original *Red* album?

✓ OR ✗

26. Which child's voice appears in the opening of 'Gorgeous'?

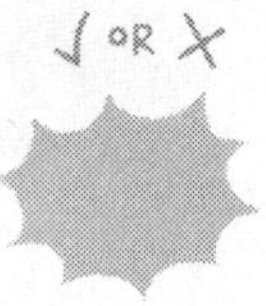

A. ____________________

√ OR X

27. Which famous couple is referenced in '... Ready For It?'?

A. ____________________

√ OR X

28. Whose tattoos do those on Taylor's face replicate in the 'Fortnight' music video?

A. ____________________

√ OR X

29. Finish this lyric from 'The Alchemy', TTPD: 'Where's the trophy? ________

________ ________ ________,

________ ________ ________

30. What age does Taylor reference turning in her 10 Minute Version of 'All Too Well' on *Red (TV)*?

✓ OR ✗

A. __________________________________

31. Which Taylor song features The Chicks?

✓ OR ✗

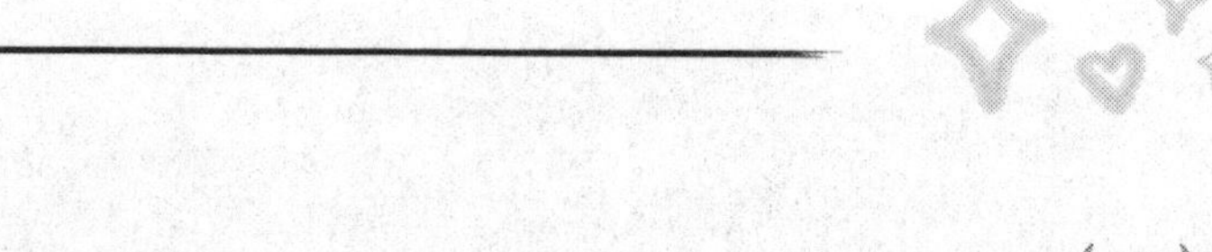

A. __________________________________

32. Which *folklore* song mentions a tightrope?

✓ OR ✗

A. __________________________________

33. Which renowned American socialite did Taylor write about in 'the last great american dynasty'?

√ OR X

A. ______

34. Which names are mentioned in 'betty'?

√ OR X

35. Which Kanye West song is about Taylor?

√ OR X

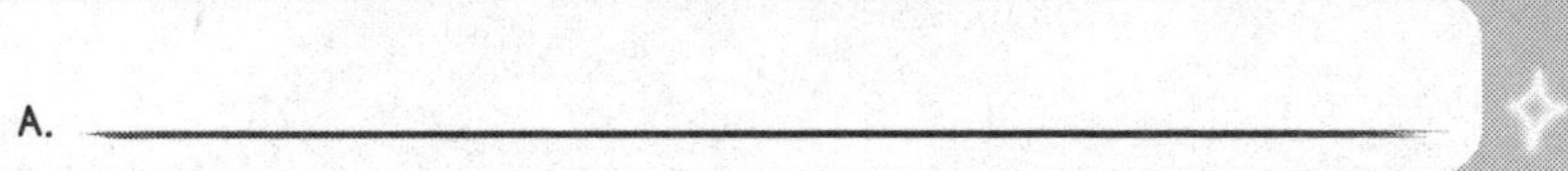

36. In late 2014 Taylor controversially pulled her music from where?

✓ OR ✗

A. ______________________________

37. On which songs did Taylor collaborate with Ed Sheeran?

✓ OR ✗

A. ______________________________

38. Which song ends with the statement: 'I gotta have you'?

✓ OR ✗

A. ______________________________

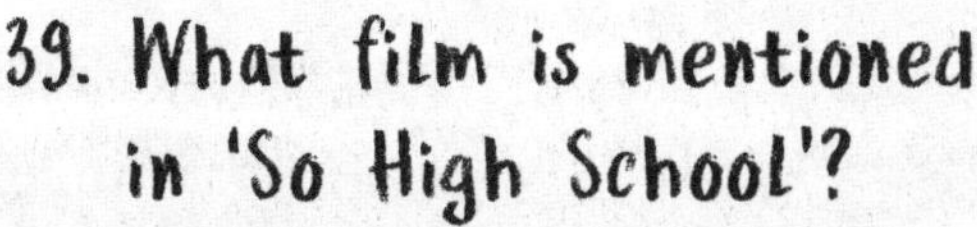

39. What film is mentioned in 'So High School'?

A CLUELESS

B TOP GUN

C AMERICAN PIE

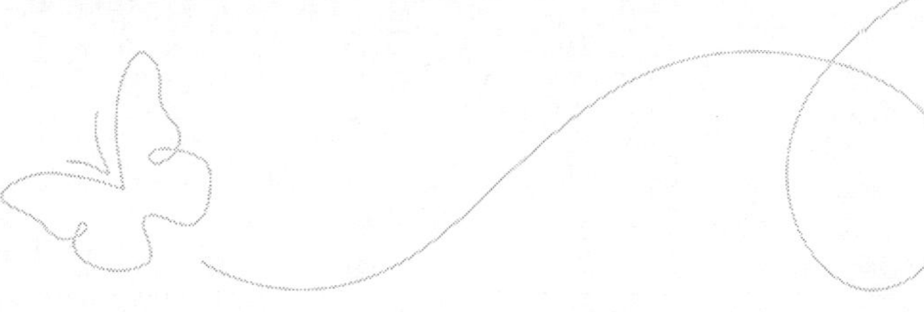

40. At 15, Taylor didn't know she'd do things greater than what?

A. ______________________________

TRACK 5

```
A A L L T O O W E L L J P D A V F X E C
M L Q Q O I A L A E D K Z V F B H J V C
G K L T P W C Q K Z G X D T M N M M E P
Q F I Y I N L M X S F S C B R P B Y C N
N C W O O O B F C K Z R E F Z M R T G F
M M Z H W U S S L R Z H M H Z E B E V D
A U X T I F H S K I O V X A H Y J A A V
D J C B O T T A D J I E P N I N A R X D
D E M O O L E H D V O A O U L Q I S A E
O C A T L K E H E T L C P W X D Y R E L
I O X R A D U R O A O S Y X M J J I Q I
M D C G J M A B A R R D O R V G D C S C
E W R S F O Y S L T S C O B C K J O V A
Q Y O G H U H W Y W E E H W Z J S C U T
H L S U F A S N V O H I K E A E J H F E
A J E P X N J F G B U K T F R S U E H D
X R P H E U V F V V I M K P X Y S T C I
Y O U R E O N Y O U R O W N K I D T V G
D S O L O N G L O N D O N R X E W R A B
L B H Z W O L K B D C I Q S F T I K K Y
```

ALL YOU HAD TO DO WAS STAY
YOU'RE ON YOUR OWN, KID
WHITE HORSE
TOLERATE IT
DELICATE
ALL TOO WELL
THE ARCHER
SO LONG, LONDON
MY TEARS RICOCHET
COLD AS YOU
DEAR JOHN

YOU SCORED

___/40!

Moving on is easy
for you to do . . .

LEVEL 6

IT'S GETTING DIFFICULT BUT IT'S REAL

1. In what year did Taylor win her first BRIT Award?

√ OR X

Ⓐ 2015

Ⓑ 2016

Ⓒ 2017

2. Why did Taylor pull her music from Spotify in 2014?

√ OR X

A. ______________________________

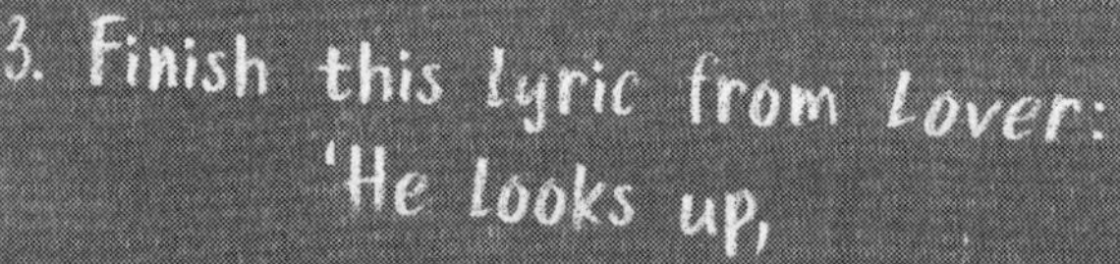

_________ _________

_________ _________,'

TRUE OR FALSE?

✓ OR ✗

4. The following celebrities all appear in the 'Bad Blood' music video: Selena Gomez, Zendaya, Hailee Steinfeld, Kendrick Lamar, Sarah Michelle Gellar, Ellie Goulding, Martha Hunt, Cara Delevingne, Ellen DeGeneres, Hayley Williams, Lena Dunham, Lily Allen, Karlie Kloss, Jessica Alba, Gigi Hadid, Mariska Hargitay, Cindy Crawford.

A. ______________________________

✓ OR ✗

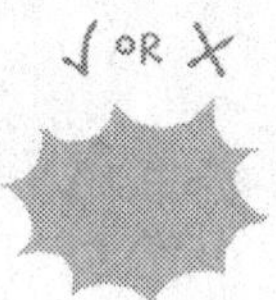

5. Which Vault song describes an experience in an antique shop?

A. ______________________________

6. What animal appears in the 'Fortnight' music video and gives its name to another *TTPD* song?

√ OR X

A. ______________________________

7. Which song from *Fearless (TV)* contains the lyric, 'No amount of freedom gets you clean'?

√ OR X

A. ______________________________

8. Which debut song did Taylor mash up with 'Bad Blood' on the *reputation* Tour?

√ OR X

A. ______________________________

9. How did Taylor meet her friend Selena Gomez?

A. ______________________________

10. In which city did Travis Kelce appear on the Eras Tour stage?

A. ______________________________

11. Which 'Speak Now' lyric is correct?

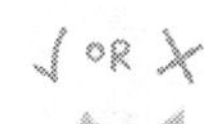

A 'AND HER SNOOTY LITTLE FAMILY ALL DRESSED IN PASTEL'

B 'AND HER SNOTTY LITTLE FAMILY ALL DRESSED IN PASTEL'

12. In the 'Anti-Hero' music video, how much money does Taylor leave to her children in her will?

A. ____________________

13. Which of these songs from *Lover* was surprise-released in 2023?

A 'ALL OF THE GIRLS YOU LOVED BEFORE'

B 'DAYLIGHT'

C 'ME!'

14. Who features on the 'Bad Blood' remix?

A. ____________________

15. What phrase does Taylor use to describe her songs that are fun, frivolous and carefree?

A. ______________________________

TRUE OR FALSE?

16. In 'Red', Taylor compares love to driving a Lamborghini down a dead-end street.

A. ______________________________

17. Which song on *folklore* is about Taylor's grandfather?

A. ______________________________

18. Which songs from *TTPD* were added to the Eras Tour setlist for the European leg in May 2024?

A. ______________________________

____

____

____

____

19. According to Taylor in 'Guilty as Sin?', what is there no such thing as?

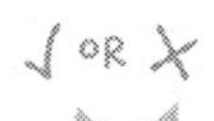

A. ______________________________

20. Which song mentions the High Line in New York City?

A. ______________________________

21. Which 'Hits Different' lyric is correct?

A 'EACH BAR PLAYS OUR FAVOURITE SONG'

B 'EACH BAR PLAYS OUR SONG'

22. Which songs did Taylor co-write with then-boyfriend Joe Alwyn?

✓ OR ✗

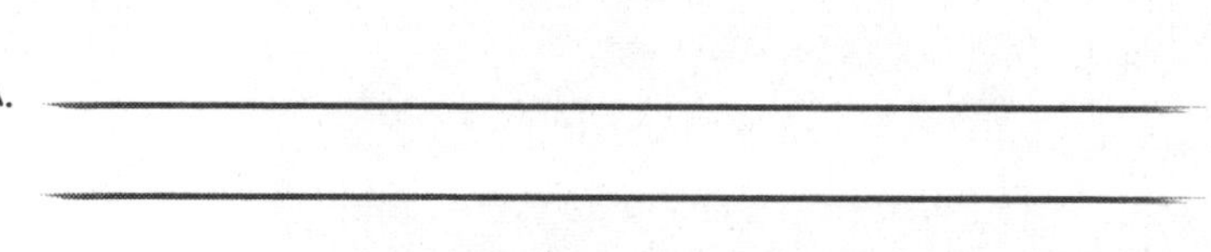

A. ____________________

23. What video game is mentioned in 'So High School'?

✓ OR ✗

A. ____________________

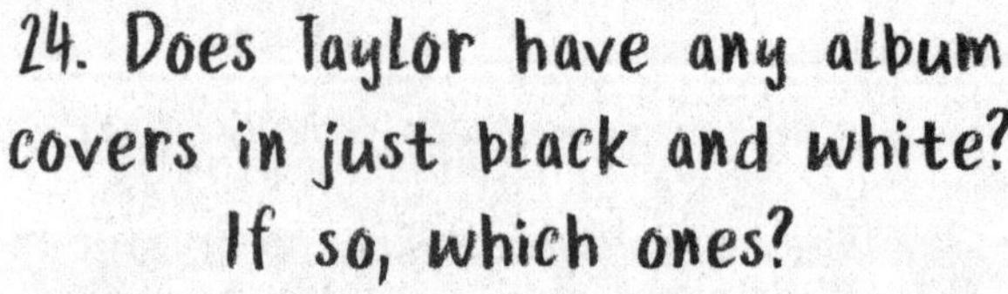

24. Does Taylor have any album covers in just black and white? If so, which ones?

A. ______________________________

____

____

25. How many songs feature on the *TTPD* double album?

√ OR X

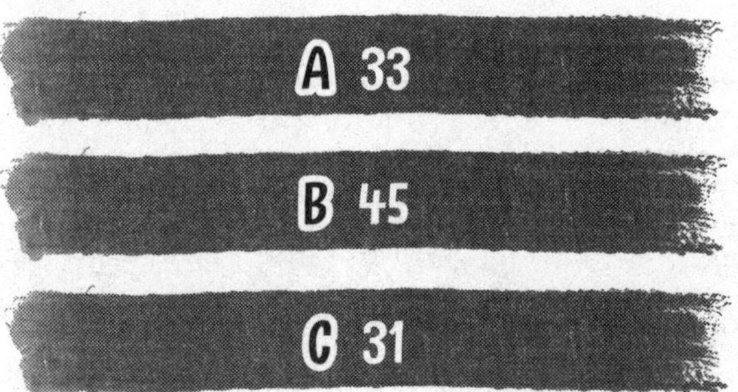

A 33

B 45

C 31

26. Which artists feature on the *Fearless (TV)* Vault tracks?

A. ______________________________

27. Which Tim McGraw song did Taylor feature on along with Keith Urban?

√ OR ✗

A. ______________________

28. Finish this lyric from *evermore*: 'I'd ________ you where the ________ ________ the ________, ________'

√ OR ✗

29. On which album does Taylor sing about non-traditional wedding rings?

√ OR ✗

A. ______________________

30. In which music video does Taylor play a cheerleader and a band geek?

√ OR X

A. ______________________________

TRUE OR FALSE?

31. Taylor is 180 centimetres tall.

√ OR X

A. ______________________________

32. Finish this lyric from *Midnights*: 'I play it __________ with the __________ of them'

√ OR X

√ OR ✗

33. Which Vault track features Keith Urban?

A. ______________________________

√ OR ✗

34. How was Taylor educated for her last few years of high school?

A. ______________________________

√ OR ✗

35. Which two Taylor songs are allegedly about John Mayer?

A. ______________________________

____

36. Which three Taylor songs contain the word 'tightrope'?

1. ______________________________
2. ______________________________
3. ______________________________

37. With which rapper did Taylor co-write 'Both of Us'?

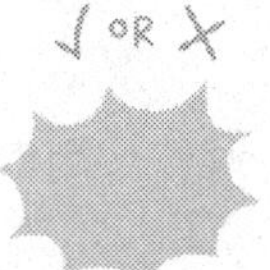

A. ______________________________

38. Finish this lyric from *TTPD*:

'You're in __________ - __________ mode, throwing __________ down __________, on __________ __________'

✓ OR ✗

39. Which band is referenced in 'The Black Dog'?

√ OR X

A THE STARTING LINE

B PANIC! AT THE DISCO

C OASIS

40. Can you name track 3 on *reputation*?

√ OR X

A. ______________________________

DECODE THE FRIENDSHIP BRACELETS

T W I L Y

A. ______________________________

____

B T R

A. ______________________________

____

M H M H M B M L

A. ______________________________

____

YOU SCORED

__ __/40!

Moving on is easy
for you to do . . .

LEVEL 7

WHO ELSE KNOWS TAYLOR LIKE YOU?

NOBODY.

1. How many Grammy Awards has Taylor won?

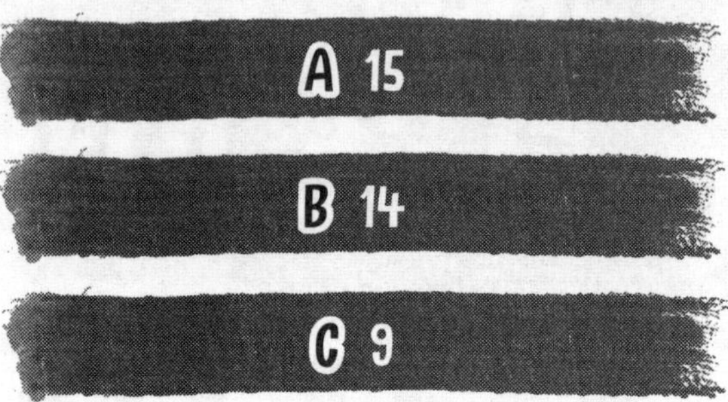

√ OR X

2. What is written on the book cover Taylor holds while lying with Post Malone in the snow in the 'Fortnight' music video?

√ OR X

A. ____________________

3. Which *TTPD* song mentions a 'crack along the wall'?

√ OR X

A. ____________________

4. What character does Taylor play in the 'Bad Blood' music video?

A. ____________________

5. Finish this lyric from Midnights: 'My town was a __________, full of __________, full of __________,'

√ OR X

6. Which classic book is referenced in 'New Romantics' and 'Love Story'?

√ OR X

A. ____________________

7. Which 'Anti-Hero' lyric is correct?

✓ OR ✗

A 'THEY COME WITH PRICES AND VICES, I END UP IN CRISIS'

B 'THEY COME WITH VICES AND PRICES, I END UP IN CRISIS'

8. What was the name of the tour Taylor had planned for 2020 but had to cancel due to the pandemic?

✓ OR ✗

A. ______________________________

9. What song did Taylor swap out early in the Eras Tour for 'the 1'?

✓ OR ✗

A. ______________________________

√ OR X

10. Finish this lyric from *Red (TV)*:
'And all I've seen since ________
________ ________, is
________ ________ and ________,
and ________ ________'

√ OR X

11. Who is the song 'Getaway Car' allegedly about?

A. ________

√ OR X

12. Taylor met actor Taylor Lautner on the set of which movie?

A. ________

13. What was the name of the school Taylor attended from the ages of 14 to 16?

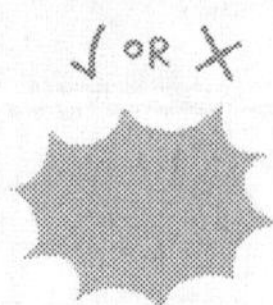

A. ______________________________

14. What is the nickname given to Taylor's 4th July parties?

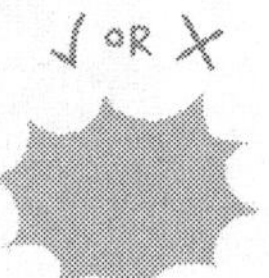

A. ______________________________

15. In the 'Karma' music video, what do Taylor's fans believe Taylor's painted nails (one blue, one black) holding a coffee cup with a clockface, relate to?

A. ______________________________

✓ OR ✗

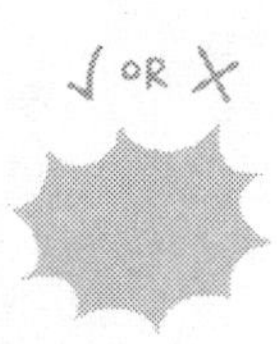

16. What are Taylor's top three highest-selling albums in the United States, in order?

1. ______________________________

2. ______________________________

3. ______________________________

17. Which two Taylor songs were on Spotify's top global songs of 2023 list for the most streams worldwide?

✓ OR ✗

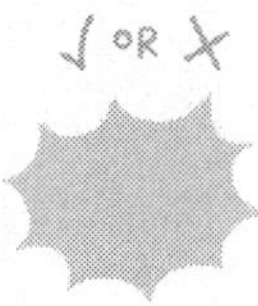

1. ______________________________

2. ______________________________

18. Which song features Gary Lightbody from Snow Patrol?

✓ OR ✗

A. ______________________________

19. Which song mentions Centennial Park?

A. ______________________________

20. Finish this lyric from 1989 (TV):
'They are the ________,
we are the ________ and we
________.'

21. Which song mentions an ex-love sipping coffee with Taylor's dad?

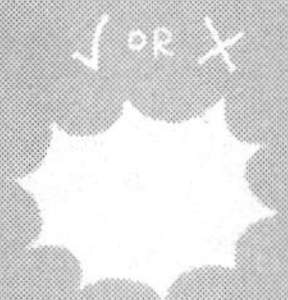

A. ______________________________

√ OR ✗

22. What is the name of the track Taylor wrote for Rihanna and Calvin Harris?

A. ______________________________

√ OR ✗

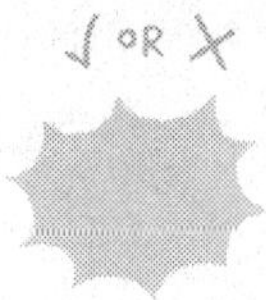

23. Which song references dancing in a storm?

A. ______________________________

24. Which *TV* re-recorded song had the most substantial changes from the original recording?

√ OR ✗

A. ______________________________

√ OR X

25. What type of shoe is mentioned in 'I Can Do It With a Broken Heart'?

A. ______________________________

26. In which song does Taylor say she's got some big enemies?

√ OR X

A. ______________________________

27. Finish this lyric from *TTPD*:
'As the men masqueraded,
I __________ __________,
__________'

√ OR X

28. Which famous music artist is name-dropped in 'Snow On The Beach'?

A. ______________________________

29. Which 'King of My Heart' Lyric is correct?

✓ OR ✗

A 'YOUR LOVE IS A SECRET I'M HOPING, DREAMING, DYING TO KEEP'

B 'YOUR LOVE IS A SECRET I'M HOPING, DREAMING, TRYING TO KEEP'

30. Which actor, daughter of a musician and Taylor squad member co-wrote 'Lavender Haze'?

A. ______________________________

31. What is the name of the beach house Taylor bought in Rhode Island?

A. ______________________

32. 'The Best Day' is dedicated to whom?

A. ______________________

33. What is the name of Taylor's autobiographical song about moving to Nashville?

A. ______________________

34. Which album did Taylor tell *Vogue* is 'a love letter to love, in all of its maddening, passionate, exciting, enchanting, horrific, tragic, wonderful glory'?

√ OR X

A. ______________________________

35. What is the longest song Taylor has written?

√ OR X

A. ______________________________

36. Finish this lyric: 'I'll be 87, __________ __________ __________ __________'

√ OR X

TRUE OR FALSE?

37. Track 16 on *Speak Now (TV)* is also the name of a superhero.

A. ________________________________

38. What is the title of the duet between Taylor and Colbie Caillat?

A. ________________________________

39. Which song did American gymnast Simone Biles perform a floor routine to in 2023?

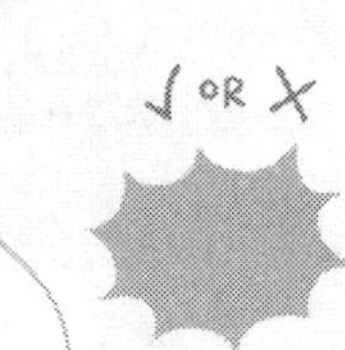

A '... READY FOR IT'

B 'STYLE'

C 'WELCOME TO NEW YORK'

40. What will Taylor stare directly at . . . but never into a mirror?

A. ____________________

VAULT TRACKS

P F I A J E C G V L E N I L M C I V N Q I L F T K
N W N V F W H E N E M M A F A L L S I N L O V E Y
T K Y O U A L L O V E R M E P D C X A Z O S T C N
A R T U F E T A H A I K I X X K D K I K L U O A M
N F Y O R O E M E W C S F K S Q Q N Z D N B U L N
T M R B W I R S J E F P I J Y D O L Y E P U M L F
X H J K X E B E Z D L P U T G Z A G X L R R G T Z
F I E F K M W E V C Z E B G O O N O K S U B Q O T
S C Z V N U R E T E A Y C E L V G U L C N A B O G
A I M U E O E P R Y R S A T T A E B N K T N A W U
Y O C E G R W W E E O W T W R T B R K T E L B E D
D T K A S I Y T D R H U I L T I E Y N A P E E L Z
O H X M N S U F H B F A T N E A C R C O V G M L S
N A J O C S A H I A Y E P H T S K T M L W E D M B
T T G Q F L E G W R T E C P I E C L O A U N P I F
G S G P B P O E E V S W B T Y N R R L U N D P N S
O W V A D C Z O Y I D T E Y L K K K U P C S K U W
P H Z C G L J P G O N D N D E Y B A U M H H H T G
D E N V U Z C P K S U A T I O B F L B Y B Y E E C
O N D R F D M Z T Q J D B Z G N A I F O G L R P E
N C Y F O O L I S H O N E O J H T B N R U Z I R R
T Y H O W F I U A Q H S Z T T I T T Y E H T G N Q
Y V D M O W Q W X M O H N Z E T Y C A V D C M S G
O C C T W G V C O T C S I P I Y L S Y L M W R E J
U T I M E L E S S N O T H I N G N E W K K V H N H

I BET YOU THINK ABOUT ME
WHEN EMMA FALLS IN LOVE
THE VERY FIRST NIGHT
NOW THAT WE DON'T TALK
ALL TOO WELL
YOU ALL OVER ME
IS IT OVER NOW
NOTHING NEW
TIMELESS

DON'T YOU
WE WERE HAPPY
I CAN SEE YOU
BYE BYE BABY
THAT'S WHEN
BABE
MESSAGE IN A BOTTLE
ELECTRIC TOUCH
RUN

MR PERFECTLY FINE
SUBURBAN LEGENDS
CASTLES CRUMBLING
FOREVER WINTER
FOOLISH ONE
BETTER MAN
SAY DON'T GO

YOU SCORED

___ ___ /40!

Moving on is easy
for you to do . . .

MONDEGREENS

Have you heard about mondegreens? They're when you think you know the lyrics to a song but realise you've been singing a slightly (or totally) different version. Even the most hardcore Swifties have been known to get some of Taylor's lines mixed up. Can you solve these mondegreens?

'BLANK SPACE' FROM *1989 (TV)*

'All the lonely Starbucks lovers'

A. ____________________

'FEARLESS' FROM *FEARLESS (TV)*

'You take my hand and drag me head first, feet last'

A. ____________________

'I KNEW YOU WERE TROUBLE' FROM *RED (TV)*

'And the stratosphere comes creepin' in'

A. ____________________

'CRUEL SUMMER' FROM *LOVER*

'He looks so pretty, like the devil'

A. ____________________

'BEJEWELED' FROM *MIDNIGHTS*

'And I miss you, but I miss Spider-Man'

A. ____________________

'I BET YOU THINK ABOUT ME' FROM *RED (TV)*

'Chasing maple leaf status, last time you felt free'

A. ______________________________

____

'OUR SONG' FROM *TAYLOR SWIFT*

'Our song is as slim as green doors'

A. ______________________________

'WILDEST DREAMS' FROM *1989 (TV)*

'He's so dull and handsome as hell'

A. ______________________________

'STYLE' FROM *1989 (TV)*

'Fake interview, oh, It's been a while since I have even heard from you'

A. ______________________________

____

____

'I WISH YOU WOULD' FROM *1989 (TV)*

'To stand back wasted'

A. ______________________________

LEVEL 8

THESE LINGERING QUESTIONS KEEP YOU UP

1. What is the name of the first song Taylor ever wrote?

√ OR X

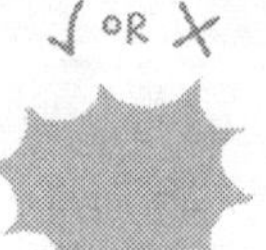

A 'LUCKY ME'

B 'LUCKY YOU'

C 'LUCKY US'

TRUE OR FALSE?

2. Taylor has been nominated for one Golden Globe Award.

√ OR X

A. ____________________

3. With which legendary composer did Taylor co-write a song for the movie *Cats*?

√ OR X

A. ____________________

4. In the 'I Can See You' music video, what is the significance of the dress and piano behind Taylor Lautner in the fight scene?

√ OR X

A. ______________________________

5. Finish this lyric from *reputation*: 'You don't need to __________ me, but would you __________ __________ with me?'

√ OR X

6. Which former US First Lady presented Taylor with The Big Help Award at the Kids' Choice Awards?

√ OR X

A. ______________________________

TRUE OR FALSE?

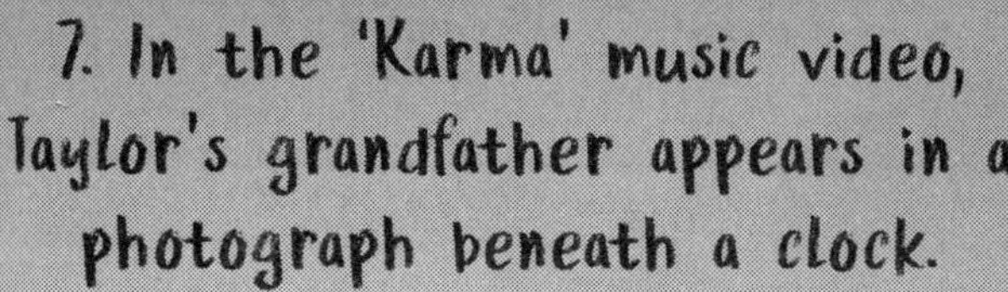

7. In the 'Karma' music video, Taylor's grandfather appears in a photograph beneath a clock.

A. ____________________

✓ OR ✗

8. Finish this lyric from *Taylor Swift*: 'Take me back when ________ ________ ________ ________ ________ ________.'

✓ OR ✗

9. In which two songs is Shakespeare's *All's Well That Ends Well* mentioned?

A. ____________________

✓ OR ✗

10. Which 'Chloe or Sam or Sophia or Marcus' lyric is correct?

✓ OR ✗

A 'IF YOU WANT TO BREAK MY COLD, COLD HEART'

B 'IF YOU WANT TO BREAK MY COLD, HARD HEART'

11. What is printed on the badge Taylor wears in the 'Anti-Hero' music video?

✓ OR ✗

A. ______________________________

12. How many back-up singers join Taylor on stage for the Eras Tour?

✓ OR ✗

A. ______________________________

13. Which songs were dropped to accommodate new songs from *TTPD* into the Eras Tour and from which eras?

✓ OR ✗

A. ______________________________

____

____

____

____

____

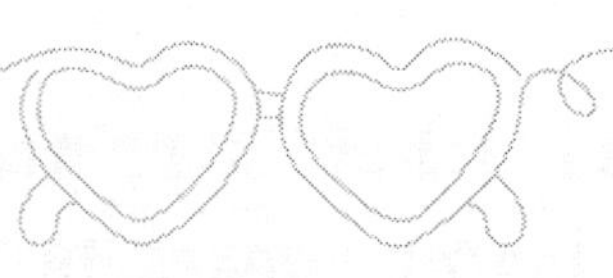

14. Which F1 driver was Taylor rumoured to be dating in 2023?

✓ OR ✗

A FERNANDO ALONSO

B LEWIS HAMILTON

C CARLOS SAINZ

15. Which singer described Taylor as 'the most iconic pop woman of our generation'?

A. ______________________________

TRUE OR FALSE?

16. Taylor wrote one song for the *Hannah Montana: The Movie* soundtrack.

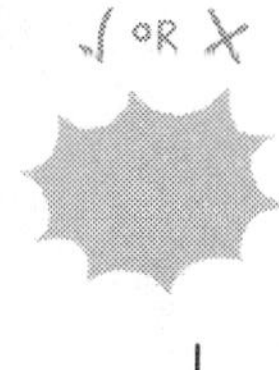

A. ______________________________

17. With which actor and former co-star did Taylor sing a duet on the *Ellen* show?

A. ______________________________

18. What did Taylor say at the Eras Tour is her favourite colour?

√ OR X

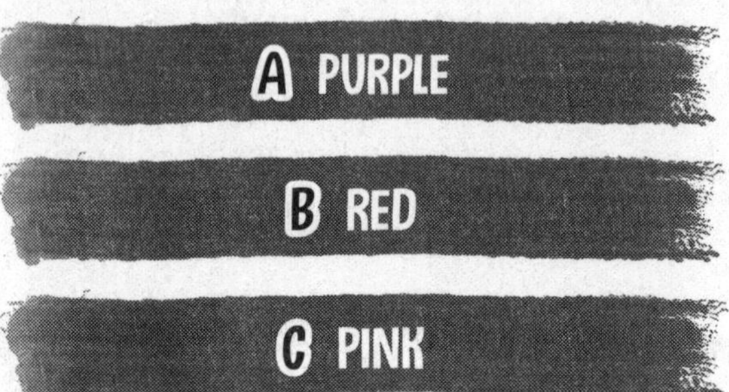

19. Which *Speak Now (TV)* song mentions a tightrope?

√ OR X

A. ______________________________

20. Which song did Taylor release with T-Pain?

√ OR X

A. ______________________________

√ OR X

21. Finish this lyric from *evermore*:
'You got ________ ________
since you left ________'

√ OR X

22. As of November 2023, what were Taylor's top three most-streamed songs on Spotify?

1. ________
2. ________
3. ________

√ OR X

23. What are Taylor's two longest song titles?

A. ________

____

____

____

24. Which suburb of Nashville, Tennessee, did the Swift family move to when Taylor was a teenager so she could pursue her music career?

✓ OR ✗

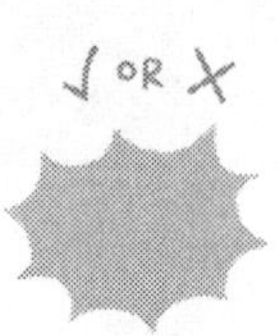

A. ____________________

25. Finish this lyric from *Lover*: 'I saw the ________ first and then I heard the ________.'

✓ OR ✗

26. Which One Direction song is rumoured to have been written about Taylor?

✓ OR ✗

A. ____________________

27. What colour eyes are mentioned in 'State Of Grace'?

√ OR X

Ⓐ BLUE

Ⓑ GREEN

Ⓒ HAZEL

28. In which song does Taylor name-check Stevie Nicks?

√ OR X

A. ____________________

29. Finish this lyric from Midnights:
'From ________ ________ to ________ ________ I waited ages to ________ , ________ ________

√ OR X

30. Under which pseudonym did Taylor write when working with then-boyfriend Calvin Harris?

A. ______________________________

✓ OR ✗

31. What truck did the boy in 'Tim McGraw' drive?

A. ______________________________

32. Who was rumoured to have gifted a paper-plane necklace to Taylor?

A. ______________________________

33. Name the Vault songs from *Speak Now (TV)*.

A. ______________________________

____

____

____

____

____

34. Which season is referenced in 'You're On Your Own, Kid'?

A. ______________________________

35. Which two songs use the term 'casually cruel'?

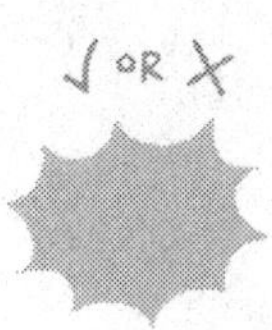

A. ______________________________

36. Taylor performed at which major sporting event in 2016?

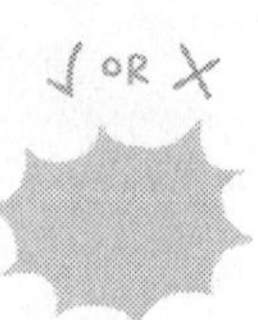

A. ______________________________

37. In which year did Taylor make her acting debut in a major film?

A. ______________________________

38. What song was inspired by the Netflix film *Someone Great*?

A. ______________________________

39. How many singles from *1989* reached number 1 in Australia, the UK and the US? Can you name them?

A. ______________________________

____

____

✓ OR ✗

40. Finish this lyric from *TTPD*:
'Lost to the
__________ __________
chapter of your life'

DECODE THE FRIENDSHIP BRACELETS

I B Y T A M

A. ______________________

____

L W Y M M D

A. ______________________

____

A Y H T D W S

A. ______________________

____

YOU SCORED

___/40!

Moving on is easy
for you to do . . .

13

LEVEL 9

YOU CAN BUILD A CASTLE OUT OF ALL THE THINGS YOU KNOW ABOUT TAYLOR SWIFT

√ OR ✗

1. Which Taylor Swift music video features *Top Gun: Maverick* star Miles Teller?

A. ______________________________

√ OR ✗

2. Which character did Taylor play in *Cats*?

A. ______________________________

3. Finish this (new) lyric from *Red (TV)*: 'You kept me like ________ ________, but I kept you like ________ ________.'

√ OR ✗

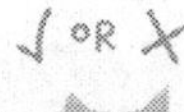

4. Which haute couture design house created the sequinned bodysuits Taylor wears in the *Lover* set of her Eras show?

A. ______________________________

5. How many Taylors appear in the final scene of the 'Look What You Made Me Do' music video?

A. ______________________________

6. What year did Taylor date Joe Jonas?

A. ______________________________

7. What was the name of Taylor's first fragrance?

✓ OR ✗

A WONDERLOVE

B WONDERSTRUCK

C WONDERLUST

8. Finish this lyric from 1989 (TV):
'Being this ________
is ________'

✓ OR ✗

9. From which Charles Dickens novel does Taylor rework the opening line to open 'Getaway Car'?

✓ OR ✗

A. ________________

TRUE OR FALSE?

✓ OR ✗

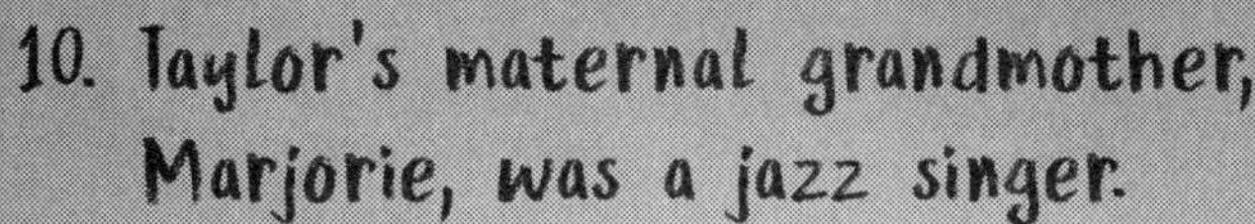

10. Taylor's maternal grandmother, Marjorie, was a jazz singer.

A. ______________________________

✓ OR ✗

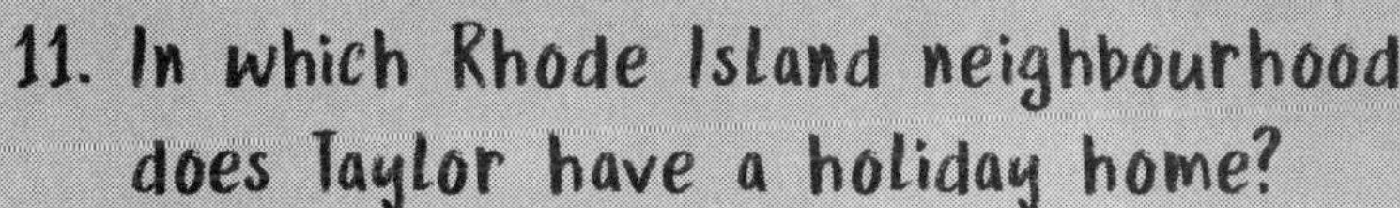

11. In which Rhode Island neighbourhood does Taylor have a holiday home?

A. ______________________________

12. Which 'The Bolter' lyric is correct?

✓ OR ✗

A 'BUT IT ALWAYS ENDS UP IN A TOWN CAR SPEEDING, OUT THE DRIVE ONE EVENING'

B 'BUT IT ALWAYS ENDS UP WITH A TOWN CAR SPEEDING, OUT THE DRIVE ONE EVENING'

13. Which *Speak Now (TV)* Vault track had a music video filmed in Liverpool?

A. ____________________________________

14. With which band did Taylor co-write 'Two is Better Than One'?

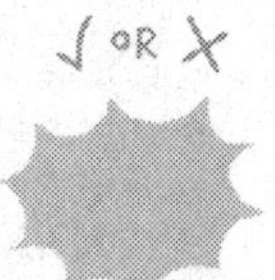

A. ____________________________________

15. Can you name five Taylor songs that have a number in their title?

A. ____________________________________

____

____

____

____

16. What is the name of the song John Mayer is rumoured to have written about Taylor?

A. ____________________

17. How did Taylor describe what the humidity had done to her hair when she performed in Singapore on the Eras Tour?

A. ____________________

18. In which song do the lyrics reference Taylor's eating disorder?

A. ____________________

19. How many witchy remixes of 'willow' are there?

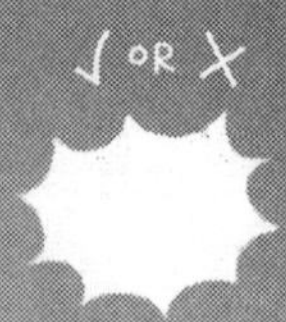

A. ____________________

20. Which 'Back to December' lyric is correct?

√ OR X

A 'YOU GAVE ME ROSES, AND I LEFT THEM THERE TO DIE'

B 'YOU GAVE ME FLOWERS, AND I LEFT THEM THERE TO DIE'

√ OR X

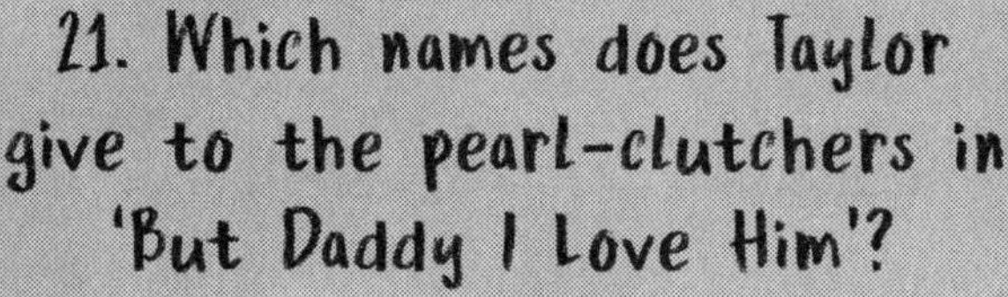

21. Which names does Taylor give to the pearl-clutchers in 'But Daddy I Love Him'?

A. ____________________

22. Which hotel does Taylor mention in 'The Tortured Poets Department'?

✓ OR ✗

A. ______________________________

23. Which fairytale is referenced in 'The Best Day'?

✓ OR ✗

A. ______________________________

24. How much time passed between the release of 1989 and 1989 (TV)?

✓ OR ✗

A. ______________________________

25. Can you name all the songs Taylor released from The Vault for *Red (TV)*?

✓ OR ✗

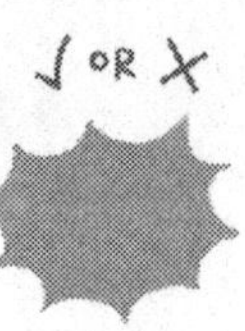

A. ______________________________

____

____

____

____

____

____

____

____

26. Finish this lyric from *folklore*: 'You had to ________ me, but it ________ you just the same'

✓ OR ✗

27. Who did Taylor sing about in 'Mary's Song'?

√ OR X

A. ______________________________

28. Which Charli XCX song on the album *brat* have fans speculated could be about Taylor?

√ OR X

A. ______________________________

29. What is the name of Taylor's second fragrance?

√ OR X

A. ______________________________

30. Taylor performed which song at the 2013 Victoria's Secret Fashion Show?

√ OR X

A. ______________________________

31. Which song is Taylor not sure she'll ever perform live?

√ OR X

A. ______________________________

32. What are Taylor's back-up dancers on the Eras Tour called?

√ OR X

A. ______________________________

33. In which song is Taylor left standing in her party dress?

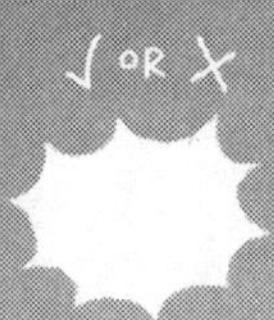

A. ______________________________

34. Finish this lyric from *TTPD*:
'I'm seeing visions, Am I ________?
Or ________? Or ________?'

35. Which Olivia Rodrigo song have fans speculated could be about Taylor?

A. ______________________________

36. Finish this lyric from *evermore*: 'Telling all the ________ ________ anything they ________ ________.'

✓ OR ✗

37. Which song from *1989 (TV)* references Nathaniel Hawthorne's classic book *The Scarlet Letter*?

✓ OR ✗

A. ____________________

38. The EP *Beautiful Eyes* was released exclusively in which US stores?

✓ OR ✗

A. ____________________

39. In which crime drama series did Taylor appear as a guest in 2009?

A. ______________________________

40. Which lyric from 'The Albatross' is correct?

√ OR X

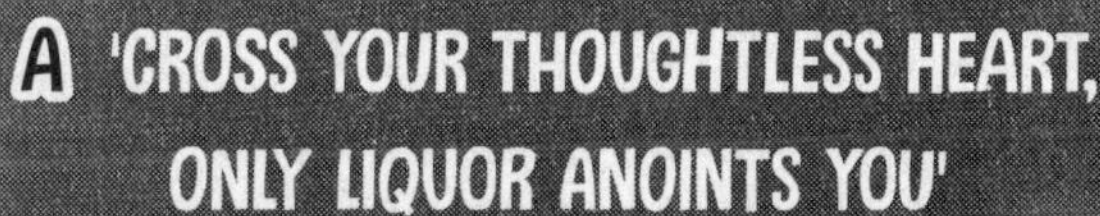

A 'CROSS YOUR THOUGHTLESS HEART, ONLY LIQUOR ANOINTS YOU'

B 'CROSS YOUR THOUGHTLESS HEART, ONLY LIQUID ANOINTS YOU'

C A C L D O J Z R A T C J H Q
A M O U B M A G V Z A H O A D
L A N C N I K B Q R Y G E R T
V T O P O X E W J T L B J R R
I T R O T R G L X L O D O Y A
N Y K Y L J Y T C J R F N S V
H H E S U O L M X O L I A T I
A E N Z C E L Z O H A O S Y S
R A N T A A E G N N U J B L K
R L E O S L N D P M T L K E E
I Y D B T W H B C A N E K S L
S K Y D I Y A X S Y E D I K C
D T E A L N A I Z E R G N T E
A K U P L P L L O R Y R C M H
T O M H I D D L E S T O N R C

JAKE GYLLENHAAL
CORY MONTEITH
JOE ALWYN
HARRY STYLES
JOE JONAS
TAYLOR LAUTNER
CONOR KENNEDY
JOHN MAYER
MATTY HEALY
TOM HIDDLESTON
TRAVIS KELCE
CALVIN HARRIS
LUCAS TILL

YOU SCORED ___/40!

Moving on is easy
for you to do . . .

A LOT
GOING ON
AT THE
MOMENT

LEVEL 10

I BET YOU THINK ABOUT TAYLOR SWIFT (A LOT)

1. Finish this lyric from *Lover*:
'So cut the ________,
summer's a ________'

√ OR X

TRUE OR FALSE?

2. 'Guilty as Sin?', 'The Prophecy' and 'Now That We Don't Talk' include Biblical references.

A. ________

√ OR X

3. What line in 'Long Story Short' refers to *Alice's Adventures in Wonderland*?

√ OR X

A. ________

____

4. Which *TTPD* song references William Shakespeare's *Romeo and Juliet*?

A. ______________________________

5. Which *High School Musical* actor starred alongside Taylor in *The Lorax*?

- **A** VANESSA HUDGENS
- **B** ASHLEY TISDALE
- **C** ZAC EFRON

6. Finish this lyric from *1989 (TV)*:
'Like any real love, it's
__________ __________'

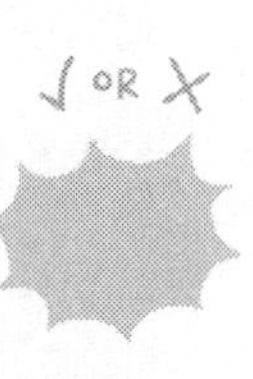

7. Which band did Taylor open for in 2008 on the Me and My Gang Tour?

A. ______________________________

8. Which 'this is me trying' lyric is correct?

A 'AND MY WORDS SHOOT TO KILL WHEN I'M MAD'

B 'AND MY WORDS AIM TO KILL WHEN I'M MAD'

9. How many wardrobe changes does Taylor have every Eras Tour performance?

A. ______________________________

10. What year did Taylor date Jake Gyllenhaal?

A. ____________________________________

11. Finish this lyric from *Midnights*: 'I want the __________ of your heart'

12. In her Vogue '73 Questions', which award did Taylor keep next to her coffee machine?

A. ____________________________________

13. What is Taylor's favourite TV show?

A. ____________________

√ OR X

14. Finish this lyric from *Fearless (TV)*: 'After everything and that little ________ ________'

TRUE OR FALSE?

15. Taylor has written three songs with Robbie Williams.

A. ____________________

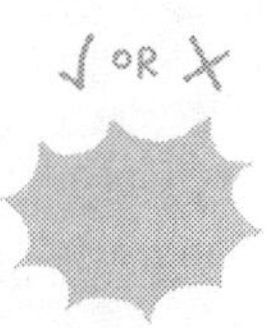

16. Finish this lyric from TTPD:
'Now I want to sell my house and
________ ________ ________
________ ________ ________'

17. With which singer did Taylor co-write 'Babe'?

A. ________________________________

18. What colour eyes does Taylor mention in 'Sparks Fly'?

A. ________________________________

19. Finish this lyric from *reputation*: 'And there are no rules when you _______ _______ here, _______ _______ _______ the chandelier'

✓ OR ✗

20. What is Stevie Nicks' favourite Taylor song, which Taylor played acoustic on piano for Nicks during the Eras Tour?

A. ______________________________

21. Which two songs include the phrase 'Fake it till you make it'?

✓ OR ✗

A. ______________________________

____

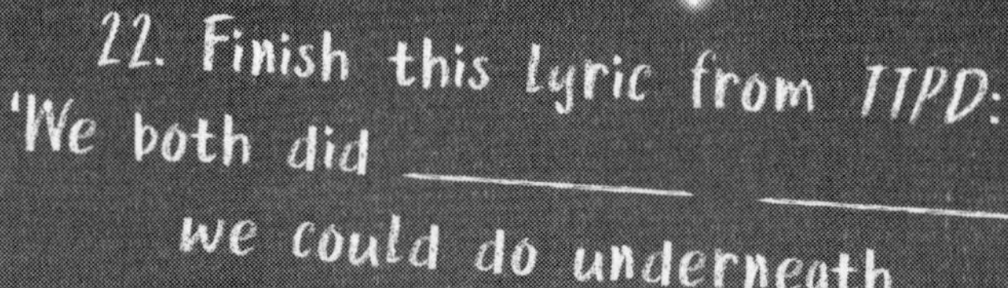

22. Finish this lyric from *TTPD*: 'We both did ________ ________ we could do underneath ________ ________ ________.'

✓ OR ✗

23. What Katy Perry diss track is allegedly about Taylor?

✓ OR ✗

A. ________________________________

24. Finish this lyric from *1989 (TV)*: 'High tide came and ________ ________ ________.'

✓ OR ✗

25. Which song did Taylor write after being inspired by a talk with Lena Dunham?

√ OR X

A. ____________________

26. Which 'Mr Perfectly Fine' lyric is correct?

A 'AND I NEVER GOT PAST WHAT YOU PUT ME THROUGH'

B 'AND I NEVER GOT PAST WHAT YOU DRAGGED ME THROUGH'

√ OR X

27. What is the name of the character Taylor voices in the animated film *The Lorax*?

√ OR X

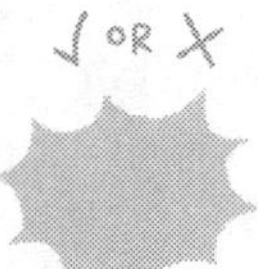

A. ____________________

√ OR ✗

28. Which music video did Taylor film at Cumberland University?

A. ____________________

√ OR ✗

29. Finish this lyric from *reputation*:

'__________ __________ __________

__________ __________ __________

__________, I do it all the time'

√ OR ✗

30. What songs did Taylor write for the *Hannah Montana* soundtrack?

A. ____________________

31. What was the original title for the song 'The Black Dog'?

A. ______________________________

32. Which song mentions mosaic broken hearts?

A. ______________________________

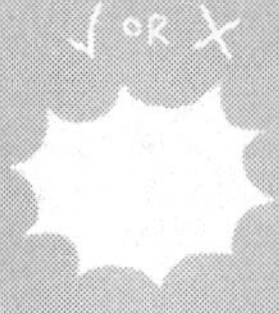

33. Finish this lyric from *1989 (TV)*: 'I broke my own heart 'cause

_______ _______ _______

_______ _______ _______,

_______'

34. In 'evermore', what is Taylor fine with?

√ OR X

A. ______________________________

35. Finish this lyric from *TTPD*: 'In the __________ of a __________ eye'

√ OR X

36. Which Marvel actor did Taylor briefly date in 2016?

√ OR X

A. ______________________________

37. What is the nickname often given to the *1989 (TV)* album?

A. ____________________

✓ OR ✗

38. In which song – and from which album – does Taylor describe love as beyond your reaches?

A. ____________________

39. Which 'The Smallest Man Who Ever Lived' lyric is correct?

√ OR X

A 'YOU CRASHED MY PARTY AND MY RENTAL CAR'

B 'YOU CRASHED MY PARTY AND YOUR RENTAL CAR'

TRUE OR FALSE?

√ OR X

40. Taylor set both 'Lover' and 'Peter' to a waltz.

A. ______________________________

DECODE THE FRIENDSHIP BRACELETS

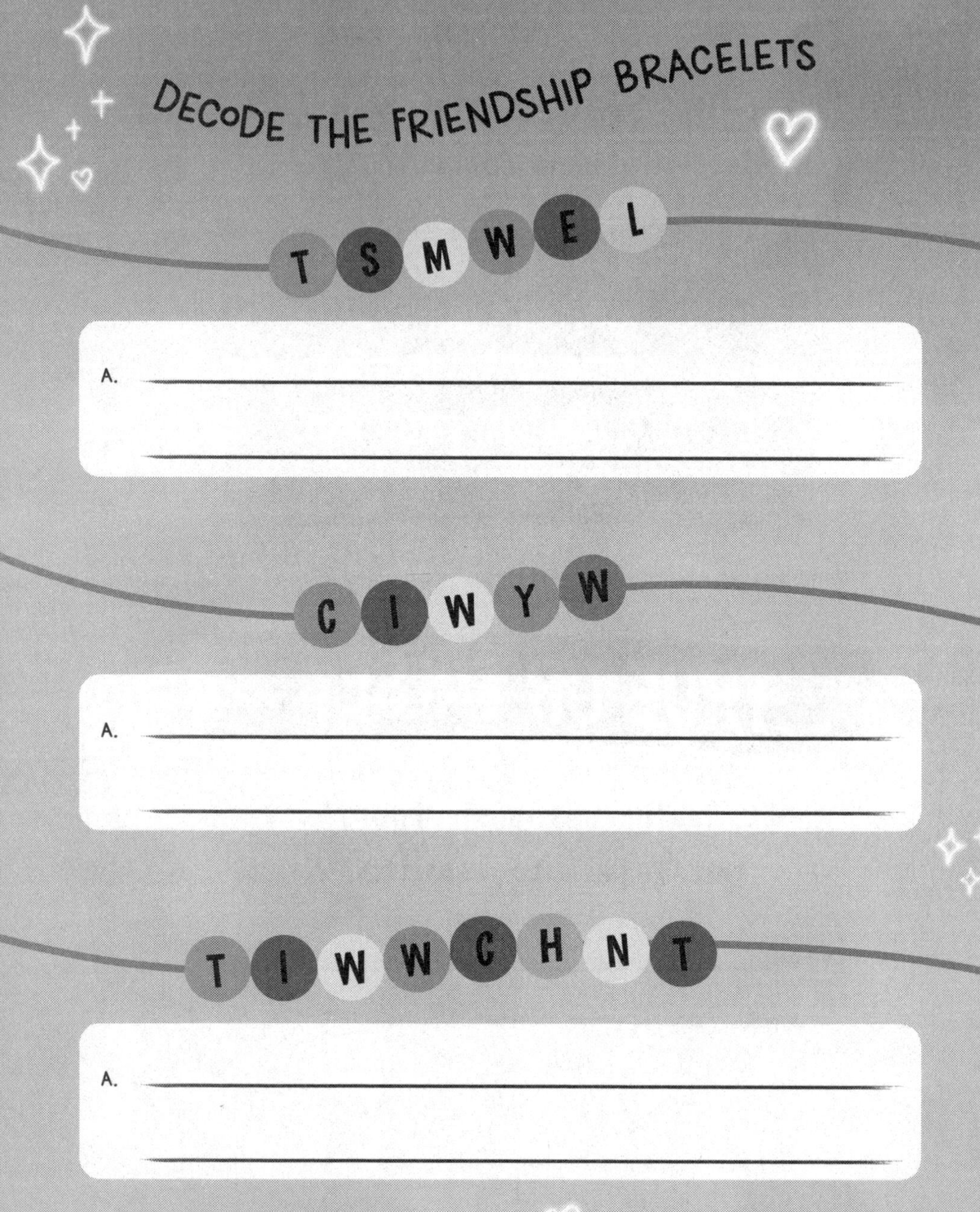

YOU SCORED ___/40!

Moving on is easy for you to do . . .

LEVEL 11

YOU ARE DEFINED BY THE THING YOU LOVE

(TAYLOR SWIFT)

1. Which classic book is referenced in 'I Hate It Here'?

A THE SECRET GARDEN

B THE LION, THE WITCH AND THE WARDROBE

C LITTLE WOMEN

√ OR X

2. Finish this lyric: 'How dare you think it's ________, leaving me ________ and ________'

√ OR X

3. Which song is thought to be inspired by a famous character created by Nancy Mitford in *Love in a Cold Climate* and *The Pursuit of Love*?

A. ____________________

4. Which two actors feature in the music video for 'Fortnight' in *TTPD*? Why?

A. ____

____

5. How many times has Taylor appeared on *Saturday Night Live*?

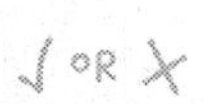

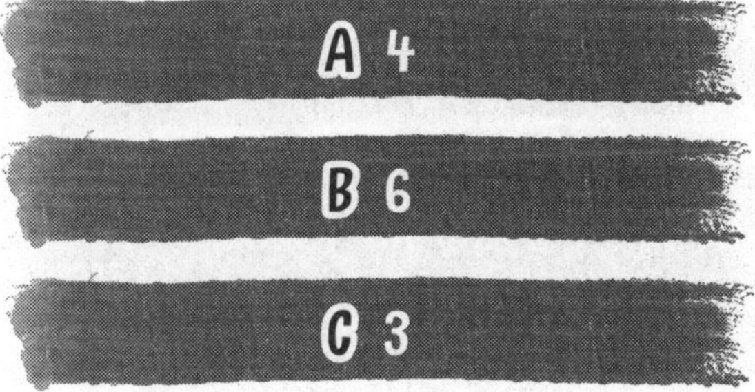

6. Taylor had a cameo in which episode of *New Girl*?

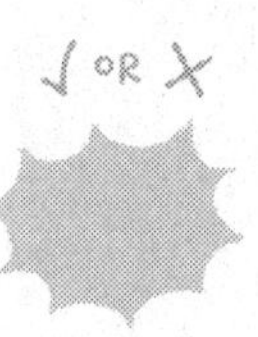

A. ____

7. Finish this lyric: '________ on the table, mine play out like ________ in a ________'

8. Which 'Florida!!!' lyric is correct?

A 'THE HURRICANE WITH MY NAME, WHEN IT CAME'

B 'THE HURRICANE HAD MY NAME, WHEN IT CAME'

9. On what date did the 2023 Eras Tour kick off?

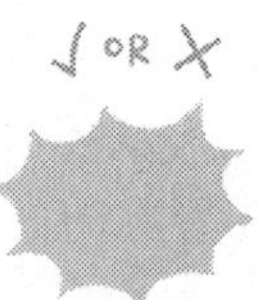

A. ________________________

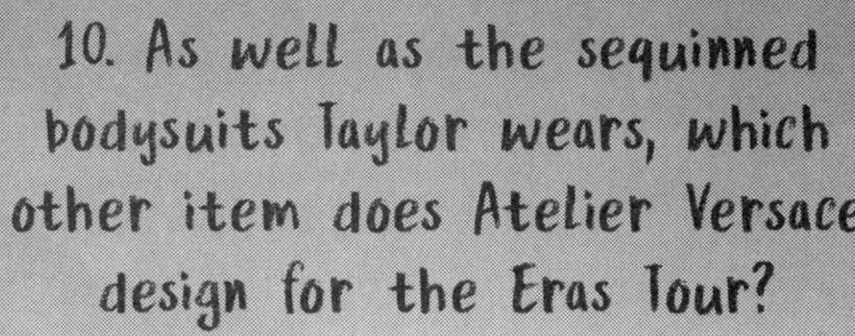

10. As well as the sequinned bodysuits Taylor wears, which other item does Atelier Versace design for the Eras Tour?

√ OR X

A. ______________________________

11. Which song did Taylor sing with Robbie Williams during the reputation Tour? At which stadium?

√ OR X

A. ______________________________

12. Finish this lyric: 'Hang your head low in ________ ________ ________ ________ ________, ________'

√ OR X

13. Fill in the blank for this quote from Taylor about her boyfriend Travis Kelce: 'This all started when Travis very adorably put me on blast on his podcast, which I thought was __________ as hell.'

√ OR X

14. Which 'Our Song' lyric is correct?

√ OR X

A 'WHEN WE'RE ON THE PHONE AND YOU TALK REAL LOW'

B 'WHEN WE'RE ON THE PHONE AND YOU TALK REAL SLOW'

15. Taylor is godmother to her friend Jaime King's son; what is his name?

√ OR X

A. ______________________________

√ OR X

16. Finish this lyric: 'Let's fast forward to 300 ________ ________, ________ ________'

√ OR X

17. Which song did Taylor sing with Bryan Adams during the *reputation* Tour?

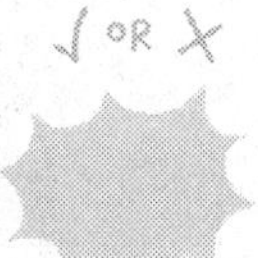

A. ____________________

√ OR X

18. Finish this lyric: 'Say you fancy me, not ________ ________'

19. Which famous English actor described his ideas for a date, which appear as the voice intro to 'London Boy'?

√ or X

A. ____________________

20. For which movie did Taylor write and perform 'Sweeter Than Fiction'?

√ or X

A. ____________________

21. Which Beatles track did Taylor perform with Paul McCartney on a 2015 edition of *Saturday Night Live*?

√ or X

A. ____________________

22. Which song mentions Taylor's namesake?

A. ______________________________

23. Finish this lyric: 'Now I'm ________ ________ ________ in the story of your life'

✓ OR ✗

24. Which American poet is Taylor reported to be distant cousins with?

A. ______________________________

25. Finish this lyric: 'You keep his shirt, ______ ______, ______ ______.'

✓ OR ✗

26. Which famous American political couple is 'Starlight' about?

✓ OR ✗

A. ______________________________

27. Which classic novel is visually referenced when Taylor blows up to giant size in the 'Anti-Hero' music video?

✓ OR ✗

A. ______________________________

28. Who plays Prince Charming in the 'Bejeweled' music video?

√ OR X

A. ____________________

29. Finish this lyric: 'One less temptress, one less __________ to __________'

√ OR X

30. What colour skirt is mentioned in 'imgonnagetyouback'?

√ OR X

A. ____________________

31. What was Taylor searching for in 'Welcome To New York'?

A. ______________________________

32. What Cher quote is displayed in the 'You Need To Calm Down' music video?

A. ______________________________

33. What is the name of the original song Taylor wrote for the *Cats* soundtrack?

A. ______________________________

34. What is the name of Taylor's first live album?

A. ______________________________

35. Which warrior from Greek mythology is referenced in 'State Of Grace'?

✓ OR ✗

A HERACLES

B ACHILLES

C PERSEUS

36. When did Taylor perform with Nicki Minaj?

A. ______________________________

37. Can you name all the *Fearless (TV)* Vault songs?

A. ________________________________

38. Which song from *Red (TV)* mentions calling someone up at different times in the early morning?

A. ________________________________

39. Which artists did Taylor collaborate with on 'Highway Don't Care'?

√ OR X

A. ______________________________

40. Which song mentions Taylor's lost love forgetting to turn his location off?

√ OR X

A. ______________________________

COLLABORATORS

K Q Q T K I J D T P F Y E Y N L P H S F E U H V T
E G F R E H C J N V H N K Z H K E I T H U R B A N
O T Y H T D W H F X W H X Z M D Y E T S Y I S J I
K J N T A W O S L E S D M A R E N M O R R I S O X
C F J X R Y J O H N M A Y E R C A W E I X E A I C
E T R B L Q L Y A U C E S T I M M C G R A W T E H
F L O R E N C E A N D T H E M A C H I N E F H X L
E B L M L E U P Y T G X O B Q R Y B T F J V E T K
D U E K M J P L Z W T C L G O B G G H I Z N C F E
S U A A D P Q Z Q A I F H A X B V I P P Y Q H A N
H I W W K G F R X B Y L O R N R B F V D M K I L D
E C I F B W I P B N J N L T I A V B U P R A C L R
E O Z I B U E A I C P J B I H S D R F T A T K O I
R L O C W B C Q N T V R V Z A E S E Q T U B S U C
A B N W B R S T Z Q L V G Z Q M N T L C U R T T K
N I P H O E B E B R I D G E R S S A A R Q R E B L
A E F I N N X X N H S E O V S E K M T P E B N O A
J C H B I D K S H A W N M E N D E S X I L Y I Y M
M A D T V O X T J R Y A N T E D D E R U O E R S A
S I G M E N G S O A I G B T G C X V R E S N T O R
U L F P R U P P E H K B F O R I B J E B N M A O X
A L H W X R T E J A J Q G L Q L R L L M O B T L N
M A A V X I Z D S G A R Y L I G H T B O D Y N R A
L T I I H E A Q D D F I S C Y D Q Y E V G D K O R
B J M K S X W E G P O S T M A L O N E N O K G N J

FLORENCE AND THE MACHINE
ED SHEERAN
PHOEBE BRIDGERS
HAYLEY WILLIAMS
SHAWN MENDES
KEITH URBAN
JOHN MAYER
LANA DEL REY

THE CHICKS
ZAYN
KENDRICK LAMAR
BRENDON URIE
FALL OUT BOY
GARY LIGHTBODY
POST MALONE
TIM MCGRAW
BON IVER

CHRIS STAPLETON
COLBIE CAILLAT
THE NATIONAL
RYAN TEDDER
MAREN MORRIS
FUTURE
B.O.B.
HAIM

YOU SCORED

___/40!

Moving on is easy for you to do . . .

LEVEL 12

YOU KNOW TAYLOR LIKE THE BACK OF YOUR HAND

1. Which poem is referenced in 'The Albatross'?

√ OR X

A. ____________________

2. Who taught Taylor to play the guitar?

√ OR X

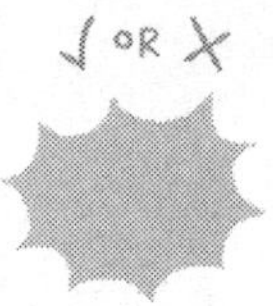

A. ____________________

3. Which three celebrities had cameos in the 'I Can See You' music video?

√ OR X

A. ____________________

____

____

4. Which of her songs did Taylor remix after she appeared in a 2009 episode of *CSI: Crime Scene Investigation*?

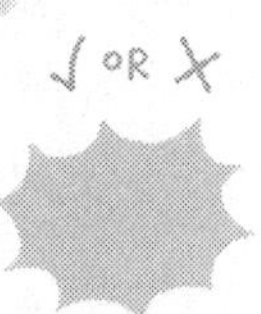

A. ______________________________

5. Finish this lyric: 'You got that ________ ________ ________ ________, white T-shirt'

6. Which song is featured in the TV series *Dickinson*?

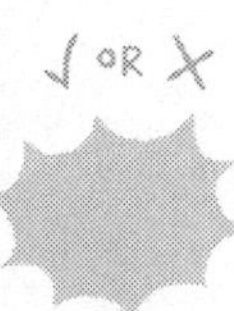

A. ______________________________

7. Finish this lyric: 'Ditch the ________, get the ________, baby, I'm the one to ________'

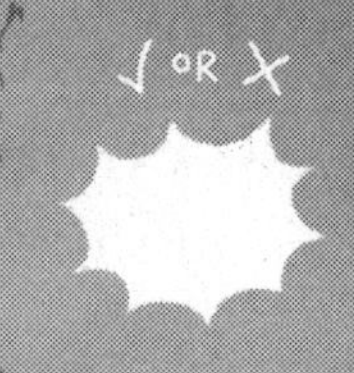

8. Which 'Snow On The Beach' lyric is correct?

✓ OR ✗

A 'STARS BY THE POCKETFUL'

B 'STARS BY THE BUCKETFUL'

✓ OR ✗

9. Finish this lyric: 'There's a ________, ________ – ________ statue of you'

10. Which 'Mary's Song' lyric is correct?

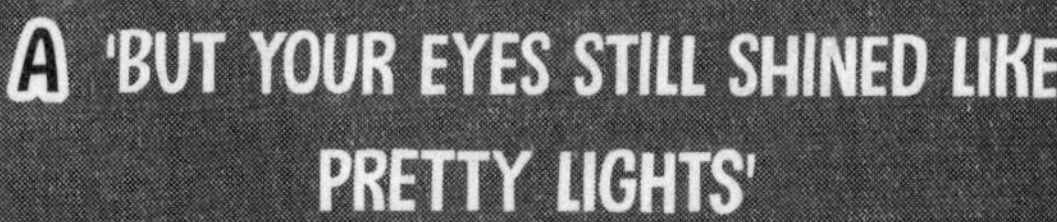

A 'BUT YOUR EYES STILL SHINED LIKE PRETTY LIGHTS'

B 'BUT YOUR EYES STILL SHINED LIKE CITY LIGHTS'

√ OR X

11. What is the name of the loafer Taylor wears for the *Red* era set in her show?

√ OR X

A. ____________________

12. How many dates are there on the Eras Tour?

√ OR X

A. ____________________

13. Finish this lyric: 'I'm ________, thanks to you'

14. Which song did Taylor teach Zac Efron to play on the guitar?

A. ____________________

15. What is the name of the novel Taylor wrote when she was 14?

A. ____________________

16. Which Dave Matthews Band song did Taylor cover in 2011?

A. ______________________

17. Finish this lyric: '______ ______ ______ ______ ______ time could never mend'

18. Which song did Taylor perform with Mick Jagger during the *1989* World Tour?

A. ______________________

19. In which city, state and country did the 2023 Eras Tour kick off?

A. ____________________

20. Finish this lyric: 'Are you gonna ________, ________ or ________ me?'

✓ OR ✗

21. Who directed the 'Style' music video?

A. ____________________

22. What is the name Taylor gave to the home recording studios she set up?

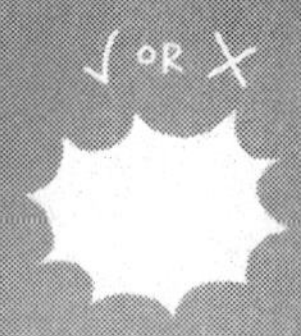

A. ______________________________

23. What is the name of Taylor's Eras Tour band?

✓ OR ✗

A. ______________________________

24. Finish this lyric: 'Bring on all the pretenders, __________, __________ __________'

✓ OR ✗

25. Who was the first music artist Taylor saw in concert?

A. ______________________________

26. Finish this lyric: '________ ________ ________ ________ ________ ________ crumbling down'

√ OR X

27. Taylor has a fear of which creature?

A. ______________________________

28. What is the necklace Taylor references in 'Out Of The Woods' and 'Is It Over Now?'

A. ______________________________

29. With which singer did Taylor co-write 'Best Days of Your Life'?

A. ______________________________

30. What date was *TTPD* released?

√ OR X

A. ______________________________

31. What did Taylor say when she broke the wrong banana off the bunch while still medicated after surgery?

A.

32. What is the shortest song Taylor has written?

√ OR X

A.

33. Taylor made her directorial debut with the music video for which song?

√ OR X

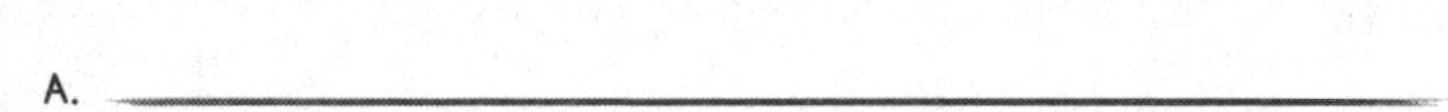

√ OR X

34. As a child, what did Taylor want to grow up to be (apart from a singer and musician)?

A. ______________________________

35. Finish this lyric: 'And you're tossing out ________, ________ ________ ________ ________, crossing out the ________ ________'

√ OR X

36. Which 1915 narrative poem by Robert Frost is referenced on 'The Outside', 'illicit affairs' and ''tis the damn season'?

A. ______________________

37. What pseudonym did Joe Alwyn use when writing songs with Taylor?

A. ______________________

38. Who plays Taylor's mother in the 'Bejeweled' music video?

A. ______________________

39. What words are written on Taylor's arm in the 'I Can See You' music video?

A. ______________________________

40. Name the four albums for which Taylor won Album of the Year at the Grammy Awards.

1. ______________________________
2. ______________________________
3. ______________________________
4. ______________________________

DECODE THE FRIENDSHIP BRACELETS

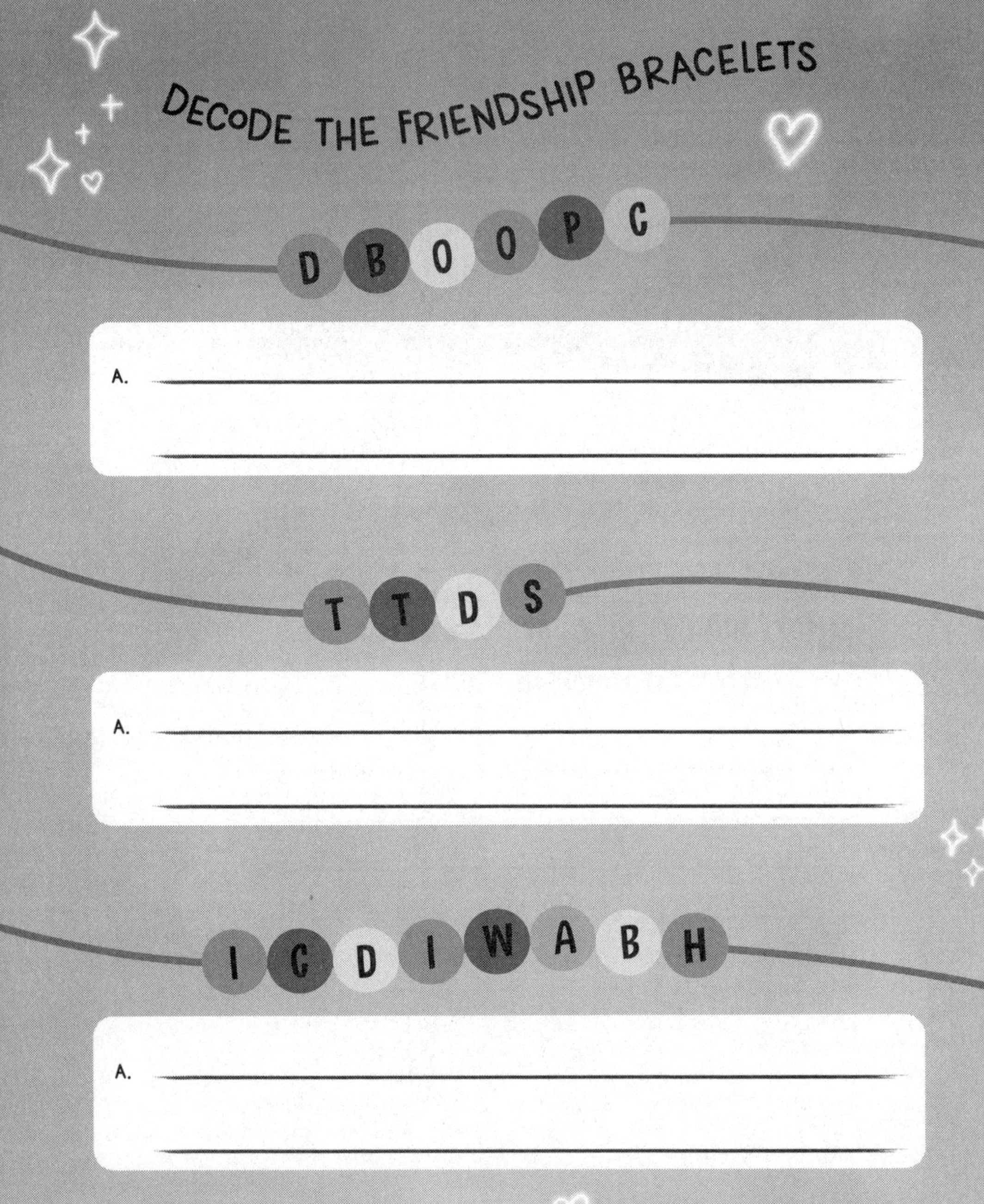

A.

A.

A.

YOU SCORED

__ __ /40!

Moving on is easy
for you to do . . .

LEVEL 13

YOU ARE A MASTERMIND

1. Which famous 1962 novel is referenced in 'So High School' and 'Hits Different'?

Ⓐ A WRINKLE IN TIME

Ⓑ A CLOCKWORK ORANGE

Ⓒ ONE FLEW OVER THE CUCKOO'S NEST

TRUE OR FALSE?

2. The title character from 'The Bolter' is also the nickname of a character in books written by British writer Evelyn Waugh in the twentieth century.

A. ____________________

√ OR ✗

3. What song did Taylor sing when she won a local talent competition when she was 11?

A. ____________________

√ OR ✗

4. Finish this lyric: 'All I know is you ________ ________ ________, You'll be ________ and I'll be ________'

√ OR ✗

5. Which music video shows Taylor ending a relationship via a phone call?

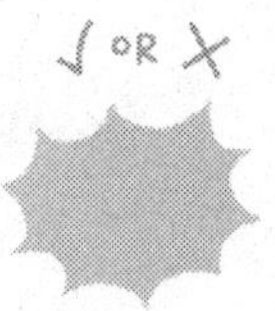

A. ____________________

6. Who produced Taylor's first studio album?

A. ______________________

7. What was Taylor's first studio album called?

A. ______________________

8. Finish this lyric: 'The __________ claimed he was a __________'

9. Which Australian designer created the white strapless dress Taylor wears in the 'Fortnight' music video?

A. ______________________

10. What is the name of the character Taylor played in the 2014 movie *The Giver*?

A ROSEMARY

B ROSIE

C ROSANNE

11. How many movies has Taylor acted in as a character other than herself? And what are they?

✓ OR X

A. ______________________________

____

____

____

____

12. What was the name of Taylor's character in *Valentine's Day*?

A. ______________________________

13. Which 'Clean' lyric is correct?

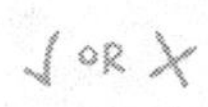

A 'AND THE SKY TURNED BLACK LIKE A PERFECT STORM'

B 'AND THE SKY TURNED BLACK LIKE THE PERFECT STORM'

14. In how many cities will Taylor perform on the Eras Tour?

A. ______________________________

15. What date did the *1989* World Tour commence?

A. ______________________________

16. Finish this lyric: 'It's a ___________, the time will come'

17. Who is the stylist for the Eras Tour?

A. ______________________________

18. What was the first song Taylor learned to play on the guitar?

✓ OR ✗

A. ______

19. Who is Taylor's make-up artist on the Eras Tour?

✓ OR ✗

A. ______

20. What is the full name of Taylor's maternal grandmother?

✓ OR ✗

A. ______

√ OR X

21. Finish this lyric: 'Were you making fun of me with some ______ ______'

√ OR X

22. What is Taylor's brother's nickname for her?

A. ______

23. Which 'Superstar' lyric is correct?

A 'SO DIM THAT SPOTLIGHT, TELL ME THINGS'

B 'SO LOWER THAT SPOTLIGHT, TELL ME THINGS'

24. What was the title of the poem Taylor wrote that won a national poetry contest?

√ OR X

A. ______________________________

TRUE OR FALSE?

25. Paul McCartney's song 'Who Cares' was inspired by Taylor.

√ OR X

A. ______________________________

26. What song did Taylor sing on the 'Hope for Haiti' album?

√ OR X

A. ______________________________

27. Who are the poets Taylor refers to in 'The Lakes'?

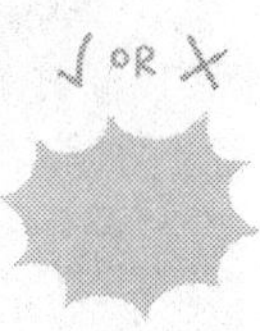

A. ______________________________

____

____

28. Finish this lyric: 'They said, Babe, you gotta _______ _______ till you _______ _______ and _______ _______.'

✓ OR ✗

29. What was the name of Taylor's first band in junior high?

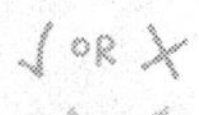

A. 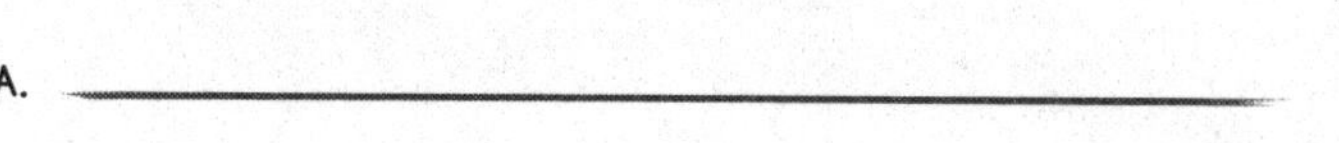

√ OR X

30. At what age did Taylor stop competitive horseback riding?

A. ______________________________

31. What day of the week did Taylor catch someone's eye?

√ OR X

A. ______________________________

√ OR X

32. What day did Taylor watch love Begin Again?

A. ______________________________

33. Can you list track five from every album?

A.

√ OR X

34. What is the Eras setlist order as of July 2024?

A.

√ OR X

35. Which children's nursery rhyme is referenced in 'The Archer'?

✓ OR ✗

A. ______________________

36. Which song mentions searching for Aurora borealis green?

✓ OR ✗

A. ______________________

37. Which song did Taylor write for Little Big Town, which won Song of the Year at the 2017 Country Music Awards?

✓ OR ✗

A. ______________________

38. Finish this lyric:
'If I was some paint did it splatter, ________ ________
________ ________ ________

39. Which song title is named after a figure from Greek mythology – the daughter of King Priam and Queen Hecuba of Troy?

A. ________________________________

40. Which F Scott Fitzgerald book is referenced in 'This Is Why We Can't Have Nice Things'?

A) THE GREAT GATSBY

B) TENDER IS THE NIGHT

C) THIS SIDE OF PARADISE

T-FOR-TAYLOR SONGS

L T M T H L N H Y T H E O T H E R S I D E O F T H E D O O R
O D H L H J Q B B O H T O D A Y W A S A F A I R Y T A L E I
Z S T I A E Y T S E S I V Q T F K Q T C T Z I L S S F M C C
W T T H S M S T F W S F S Z N U Z C G J C L M L M H S R Q D
X U H T E I J M V O X I Z I S B H B T R E A C H E R O U S T
T T P E H B S X A Q R N T J S P P S M J Y T V X V N T K P H
H H T T L E E W M L L T P H T M G T H E B L A C K D O G N E
E I O H T A T S H T L R A K E M E T L J K A A H T Q U D T M
M S L E I Z S O T Y V E O Y T V R T D F R M A K I B Z K H O
A L E A M T X T R D W T S K L H E J R L A W X B F W P L V M
N O R L E H O T G T A E E T N O E R R Y U J U S C Y T Z U E
U V A B L E R D H R U Y C A M T R A Y U I I D C B M H T T N
S E T A E B B U T E E R X A R A H S L F I N N Y Q U E H E T
C T E T S O B V H E L A E U N D N E O C I K G C F F L A L I
R L I R S L J L E F V U T D B T R W W N H R V S Q E A T L K
I M T O G T H Y M R C N C A P F H O H A G E S G C E K S M N
P G L S U E V O A Q G B M K M O A A P O Y S M T A D E W E E
T W M S F R D O N I O D C Z Y E E E V S E I P Y N G S H W W
T F T H E L A S T T I M E D M O R T C E O V L K Q I R E H N
H T I S T H E D A M N S E A S O N I S T N N E O D A G N Y M
E X H I U L G N Y B I B S R V M H E C D I I M R V M P H R Y
O V X L T U T H E P R O P H E C Y Y B A E M C Y L E A V T N
U F W S O R Y W T H E S T O R Y O F U S N P M E G I D R O U
T E S P T H A N K Y O U A I M E E Y Q A R D A C T U V Y Y X
S T H E G R E A T W A R P Q C I F K W U F F Y R G H I E O C
I H O Q D X W T Y I Y K D P N H W D B M B D Z N T R I T D U
D P R B F W G H X F B U G S N F E E C Z S V E U A M A N A D
E U E M Z T H E O N E B Z R R L R W Z H O Y W E F S E W G R
A U P J U Y Y D W H Q E E T H E A R C H E R S D Z O T N T S
E T U E T I E D T O G E T H E R W I T H A S M I L E C Y T H

TEARDROPS ON MY GUITAR
TELL ME WHY
THANK YOU AIMEE
THAT'S WHEN
THE ONE
THE ALBATROSS
THE ALCHEMY
THE ARCHER
THE BEST DAY
THE BLACK DOG
THE BOLTER
THE GREAT WAR
THE LAKES
THE LAST GREAT AMERICAN DYNASTY
THE LAST TIME
THE LUCKY ONE
THE MAN
THE MANUSCRIPT
THE MOMENT I KNEW
THE OTHER SIDE OF THE DOOR
THE OUTSIDE
THE PROPHECY
THE SMALLEST MAN WHO EVER LIVED
THE STORY OF US
THE TORTURED POETS DEPARTMENT
THE VERY FIRST NIGHT
THE WAY I LOVED YOU
THIS IS ME TRYING
THIS IS WHY WE CAN'T HAVE NICE THINGS
THIS LOVE
TIED TOGETHER WITH A SMILE
TIM MCGRAW
TIMELESS
TIS THE DAMN SEASON
TODAY WAS A FAIRYTALE
TOLERATE IT
TREACHEROUS

YOU SCORED

___/40!

Moving on is easy
for you to do . . .

ANSWERS

LEVEL 1

1. Alison
2. 13
3. 13 December 1989
4. Andrea
5. Scott
6. Austin
7. West Reading, Pennsylvania
8. Sagittarius
9. B
10. Meredith Grey, Olivia Benson, Benjamin Button
11. James Taylor
12. *Miss Americana*
13. *Taylor's Version*
14. 'music', 'mind', 'alright'
15. A
16. Kanye West
17. Red
18. *evermore*
19. Her feet
20. *Cats*
21. *reputation*
22. Friendship bracelets
23. B
24. Easter eggs
25. 'All Too Well'
26. *folklore*
27. 'angels roll their eyes'
28. B
29. *Fearless (TV)*
30. 'captain', 'bleachers'
31. B
32. TRUE
33. A
34. 'The Man'
35. 'blokes', 'benches', 'winning streak'
36. New York City
37. 'Clean'
38. 'the sun', 'the mirror'
39. *Taylor Swift*
40. A

BAD BLOOD

```
J L E N A D U N H A M W E L V I N D A G R E A T R
C F C N N P Q P S E R A Y A H H X F M U L P M A J
M X O Y S E C V U Z K V K I T M G O Q J U T X R N
E Q U T V H O M E S L I C E L E I O N K N H F S X
N X P I K W R J Z N K O Y T W S G D U E A A M Y H
L T K A R L I E K L O S S E K J I E S N D I A N O
I U Z C I N D Y C R A W F O R D H S V D X L R J M
L C C V S S E L E N A G O M E Z A T X R A E I T E
Y A M K T M O A I H X G U U A Q D R Z I K E S H S
A R A X Y H O W M C E X P Q Q C I U E C X S K E S
L A D X C F E T V Q J A D P F C D C N K B T A T I
D D L K H E I C H U C E D I X X N T D L A E H R C
R E O N E A I O R E Q A S M S M C A A A D I A I E
I L V J I L Y U R I R L T S I A X X Y M B N R N L
D E E U T D L L F I M C M A I S F L A A L F G I L
G V M S C O F E E W S S H L S C T N R R O E I T I
E I A T C M R F N Y J Z O U L T A R I K O L T Y E
K N R I U I O E N P W X H N C L R A E Q D D A U G
N G T C T N S W G W O I D V C K V O L S V Q Y Z O
O N H E T O T T M D U M L L I U E G P B S G N G U
C E A B H D B R G A E Q P L O N R R X H A P A S L
K B H I R Q Y Y P Y G Z K E I R C S F X E I R L D
O J U K O Z T D I L E M M A O A Y D E U K X X A I
U Y N Q A Y E L Z Z A V C X I A M F I R C R D Y N
T V T I T K F Y N L N D V G C O S S H X D S J Z G
```

LEVEL 2

1. Big Machine Records
2. TRUE
3. A getaway car
4. A fedora hat
5. 'this was what you wanted'
6. Post Malone
7. 13
8. Taylor
9. *folklore*
10. *Lover*
11. 'lightning'
12. *1989 (TV)*
13. TRUE
14. Dylan Thomas and Patti Smith
15. 'White Horse'
16. B
17. The Bluebird Café
18. 13 Management
19. 'scarlet letter'
20. Abigail Anderson (Berard)
21. C
22. TRUE
23. *Red (TV)*
24. There are 13 floor buttons in the lift Taylor enters.
25. 'Christmas Tree Farm'
26. B
27. *Taylor Swift*
28. 'dress'
29. *Red (TV)*
30. The Black Dog
31. 'party', 'better bodies'
32. *1989 (TV)*
33. *1989 (TV)*
34. 2006
35. B
36. Wyomissing, Pennsylvania
37. TRUE
38. James
39. Cardigan
40. B

DECODE THE FRIENDSHIP BRACELETS

1. Who's Afraid of Little Old Me?
2. You Need to Calm Down
3. We Are Never Ever Getting Back Together

LEVEL 3

1. B
2. FALSE - she was 12
3. Taylor Lautner
4. Katy Perry was a cheeseburger and Taylor was a packet of fries.
5. A tilted stage
6. Sadie Sink and Dylan O'Brien
7. 'girlfriend', 'jealous of her'
8. Alana, Danielle and Este Haim (of HAIM)
9. 'glimpse', 'legendary'
10. 'All Too Well (10 Minute Version)'
11. The *Fearless* Tour
12. Joe Alwyn
13. She ran on a treadmill while singing the entire set list.
14. FALSE - she was 20
15. B
16. 'Karma is the guy on the screen' changed to 'Karma is the guy on the Chiefs'
17. Independence Day, 4 July
18. TRUE
19. *Taylor Swift* (2006), *Fearless* (2008), *Speak Now* (2010), *Red* (2012), *1989* (2014), *reputation* (2017), *Lover* (2019), *folklore* (2020), *evermore* (2020), *Fearless (TV)* (2021), *Red (TV)* (2021), *Midnights* (2022), *Speak Now (TV)* (2023), *1989 (TV)* (2023), *THE TORTURED POETS DEPARTMENT* (2024)
20. B
21. Brendon Urie
22. 'Tim McGraw'
23. C
24. 'mad love', 'look', 'done'
25. Childless Cat Lady
26. A
27. 'You're On Your Own, Kid'
28. 'tapestry'
29. Winter and summer
30. James Dean
31. Her. She's the problem. (Hi!)
32. The Teenage Love Triangle
33. Drew
34. 'Mean'
35. 'I'll tell mine you're gay' to 'You won't mind if I say'
36. 'Shake It Off'
37. *Speak Now (TV)*
38. August
39. A
40. Midnight

SQUAD

S S H N C P N Q J A I P Z W X D V M A V V X R Y E
E M M A S T O N E L H R Q V M B E M S I S Y C I L
M H G N T L I L Y A L D R I D G E D K Y W G Y C O
X Q A S Q H U C U Y M A J R F O N W L X G K L E R
E A B I S H A D G R H A Y L E Y W I L L I A M S D
A Q I E L N C O N X J X T D N Z C G D D B K C P E
S R G G L E L E N A D U N H A M T Q A A F J R I Y
A Q A K A C E U R U A F J U V D C Z N T S A U C O
B O I W U N J S Z Z R P N Y Z A S M I S A F P E G
R A L B R C B K T H J I A I W N Z A E A D C Q L I
I V A Z A F N C G E U A A S W M T O L L I A Q A G
N R N O D I H M J U I B I Z K X M H L Z E R C L I
A I D E E B R I T T A N Y M A H O M E S S A A A H
C L E K R A K R Q S Z A F T E W L N H W I D M N A
A L R R N L A N A D E L R E Y K W H A U N E I A D
R A S A L E S T E H A I M T L S I S I F K L L H I
P V O V D O U L I L N K G M L D O N M U E E A A D
E I N I K B S O P H I E T U R N E R G K W V C I M
N G A T S V D Y I V T E D H A Z O N Z O V I A M W
T N L Z E L L I E G O U L D I N G L Y W L N B B D
E E P B B C F F E N K P H O E B E B R I D G E R S
R G G W L S U K I W A T E R H O U S E Z L N L F H
C R S F B S L S S E L E N A G O M E Z E Q E L H L
T F B L A K E L I V E L Y G F D I B I H G H O O S
D I A R F R A P F M L K E L E I G H T E L L E R G

LEVEL 4

1. Taylor Lautner
2. C
3. 'Today Was a Fairytale'
4. TRUE
5. Florence + The Machine
6. Wildest
7. She bought the Rhode Island house once owned by Harkness.
8. Dr Seuss' *The Lorax*
9. "me"
10. 'Bad Blood'
11. Best Female Video
12. Kobe Bryant
13. Republic Records, owned by Universal Music Group
14. 'blue sky', 'rain'
15. C
16. Harry Styles
17. A
18. 'Safe & Sound' and 'Eyes Open'
19. 'this', 'you'
20. Her perfect fantasy
21. 2014
22. Paris
23. 'was for all', 'momentary'
24. A
25. A crown
26. *Daylight*
27. 'Clara Bow'
28. B
29. 'the last great american dynasty'
30. The National
31. 'cages', 'mental'
32. Cornelia Street
33. Hayley Williams, Fall Out Boy
34. Max Martin and Shellback
35. 'I Don't Wanna Live Forever'
36. 'White Horse'
37. *Red*
38. Friday the 13th
39. *1989 (TV)*
40. B

DECODE THE FRIENDSHIP BRACELETS

1. You're On Your Own, Kid
2. You Belong With Me
3. I'm Only Me When I'm With You

LEVEL 5

1. TRUE
2. A
3. HERE LIES TAYLOR SWIFT'S REPUTATION
4. 'The Moment I Knew'
5. 'redhead named Abigail'
6. 'Wildest Dreams'
7. B
8. I ❤ TS
9. 'Karma'
10. A
11. The cover portrait from *Speak Now (TV)*
12. C
13. Pine Ridge Farm
14. TRUE
15. *Lover*
16. B
17. 'the less I know'
18. 'You Belong With Me'
19. FALSE - it features Ed Sheeran and Future
20. Shoes
21. Shawn Mendes
22. 'waltzing', 'rekindled flames'
23. *Taylor Swift*
24. 'cardigan' and 'Peter' both reference *Peter Pan*
25. A
26. James Reynolds, daughter of Blake Lively and Ryan Reynolds
27. Elizabeth Taylor and Richard Burton
28. They match those on collaborator Post Malone's face
29. 'He just comes running over to me'
30. 21
31. 'Soon You'll Get Better'
32. 'mirrorball'
33. Rebekah Harkness
34. Betty, Inez, James
35. 'Famous'
36. Spotify
37. 'Everything Has Changed', 'Run', 'End Game'
38. '22'
39. C
40. Date the boy on the football team

TRACK 5

```
A A L L T O O W E L L J P D A V F X E C
M L Q Q O I A L A E D K Z V F B H J V C
G K L T P W C Q K Z G X D T M N M M E P
Q F I Y I N L M X S F S C B R P B Y C N
N C W O O O B F C K Z R E F Z M R T G F
M M Z H W U S S L R Z H M H Z E B E V D
A U X T I F H S K I O V X A H Y J A A V
D J C B O T T A D J I E P N I N A R X D
D E M O O L E H D V O A O U L Q I S A E
O C A T L K E H E T L C P W X D Y R E L
I O X R A D U R O A O S Y X M J J I Q I
M D C G J M A B A R R D O R V G D C S C
E W R S F O Y S L T S C O B C K J O V A
Q Y O G H U H W Y W E E H W Z J S C U T
H L S U F A S N V O H I K E A E J H F E
A J E P X N J F G B U K T F R S U E H D
X R P H E U V F V V I M K P X Y S T C I
Y O U R E O N Y O U R O W N K I D T V G
D S O L O N G L O N D O N R X E W R A B
L B H Z W O L K B D C I Q S F T I K K Y
```

LEVEL 6

1. A
2. To protest artists not receiving compensation for their music streamed during the free trial period.
3. 'grinning like a devil'
4. FALSE: Sarah Michelle Gellar, Ellen DeGenerous and Lily Allen did not appear in this music video.
5. 'Timeless'
6. A black dog
7. 'You All Over Me'
8. 'Should've Said No'
9. They met on a double date with the Jonas brothers in 2008.
10. London
11. B
12. 13 cents each
13. A
14. Kendrick Lamar
15. 'Glitter Gel Pen' songs
16. FALSE - she compares it to driving a Maserati down a dead-end street
17. 'epiphany'
18. 'But Daddy I Love Him', 'So High School', 'Who's Afraid of Little Old Me', 'Down Bad', 'Fortnight', 'The Smallest Man Who Ever Lived', 'I Can Do It With a Broken Heart'
19. Bad thoughts
20. 'cardigan'
21. B
22. 'betty', 'exile', 'champagne problems', 'coney island', 'evermore', 'Sweet Nothing'
23. Grand Theft Auto
24. Yes, three: *reputation*, *folklore*, *THE TORTURED POETS DEPARTMENT*
25. C
26. Keith Urban, Maren Morris
27. 'Highway Don't Care'
28. 'meet', 'spirit meets', 'bones'
29. *Lover*
30. 'You Belong With Me'
31. TRUE
32. 'cool', 'best'
33. 'That's When'
34. She was homeschooled
35. 'Dear John', 'Would've, Could've, Should've'
36. 'Innocent', 'Say Don't Go', 'mirrorball'
37. B.o.B.
38. 'self-sabotage', 'spikes', 'the road'
39. A
40. 'I Did Something Bad'

DECODE THE FRIENDSHIP BRACELETS

1. The Way I Loved You
2. Better Than Revenge
3. My Heart, My Hips, My Body, My Love

LEVEL 7

1. B
2. US
3. 'Cassandra'
4. Catastrophe
5. 'wasteland', 'cages', 'fences'
6. *The Scarlet Letter* by Nathaniel Hawthorne
7. A
8. Lover Fest
9. 'invisible string'
10. 'eighteen hours ago', 'green eyes', 'freckles', 'your smile'
11. Tom Hiddleston
12. *Valentine's Day*
13. Hendersonville High School
14. Taymerica
15. The announcement months for *1989 (TV)* and *reputation*.
16. 1 *Fearless*, 2 *1989*, 3 *Taylor Swift*
17. 'Cruel Summer', 'Anti-Hero'
18. 'The Last Time'
19. 'invisible string'
20. 'hunters', 'foxes', 'run'
21. 'All Too Well (10 Minute Version)'
22. 'This Is What You Came For'
23. 'Fearless'
24. 'Girl at Home'
25. Stiletto
26. 'End Game'
27. 'hoped you'd return'
28. Janet Jackson
29. A
30. Zoë Kravitz
31. Holiday House
32. Her mother
33. 'Never Grow Up'
34. *Lover*
35. 'All Too Well (10 Minute Version)'
36. 'you'll be 89'
37. TRUE
38. 'Breathe'
39. A
40. The sun

VAULT TRACKS

```
P F I A J E C G V L E N I L M C I V N Q I L F T K
N W N V F W H E N E M M A F A L L S I N L O V E Y
T K Y O U A L L O V E R M E P D C X A Z O S T C N
A R T U F E T A H A I K I X X K D K I K L U O A M
N F Y O R O E M E W C S F K S Q Q N Z D N B U L N
T M R B W I R S J E F P I J Y D O L Y E P U M L F
X H J K X E B E Z D L P U T G Z A G X L R R G T Z
F I E F K M W E V C Z E B G O O N O K S U B Q O T
S C Z V N U R E T E A Y C E L V G U L C N A B O G
A I M U E O E P R Y R S A T T A E B N K T N A W U
Y O C E G R W W E E O W T W R T B R K T E L B E D
D T K A S I Y T D R H U J L T I E Y N A P E E L Z
O H X M N S U F H B F A T N E A C R C O V G M L S
N A J O C S A H I A Y E P H T S K T M L W E D M B
T T G Q F L E G W R T E C P I E C L O A U N P I F
G S G P B P O E E V S W B T Y N R R L U N D P N S
O W V A D C Z O Y I D T E Y L K K K U P C S K U W
P H Z C G L J P G O N D N D E Y B A U M H H H T G
D E N V U Z C P K S U A T I O B F L B Y B Y E E C
O N D R F D M Z T Q J D B Z G N A J F O G L R P E
N C Y F O O L I S H O N E O J H T B N R U Z I R R
T Y H O W F I U A Q H S Z T T J T T Y E H T G N Q
Y V D M O W Q W X M O H N Z E T Y C A V D C M S G
O C C T W G V C O T C S I P I Y L S Y L M W R E J
U T I M E L E S S N O T H I N G N E W K K V H N H
```

Mondegreens

1. 'Got a long list of ex-lovers'
2. 'You take my hand and drag me head first, fearless'
3. 'And the saddest fear comes creepin' in'
4. 'He looks up grinning, like the devil'
5. 'And I miss you, but I miss sparkling'
6. 'Chasing make-believe status, last time you felt free'
7. 'Our song is a slamming screen door'
8. 'He's so tall and handsome as hell'
9. 'Fade into view, oh, It's been a while since I have even heard from you'
10. 'To stand back where you stood'

LEVEL 8

1. B
2. FALSE - she has been nominated for two
3. Andrew Lloyd Webber
4. They are both from 'Back to December', a song Taylor wrote about . . . Taylor.
5. 'save', 'run away'
6. Michelle Obama
7. TRUE
8. 'our world was one block wide'
9. 'All Too Well (10 Minute Version)' and 'Lover'
10. A
11. VOTE FOR ME FOR EVERYTHING
12. Four
13. 'Long Live' (*Speak Now*), 'The Archer' (*Lover*), 'the 1' (*folklore*), 'the last great american dynasty' (*folklore*), ''tis the damn season' (*evermore*), 'tolerate it' (*evermore*)
14. A
15. Britney Spears
16. FALSE - she wrote two
17. Zac Efron
18. A
19. 'Innocent'
20. 'Thug Story'
21. 'shiny friends', 'town'
22. 'Blank Space', 'Cruel Summer' and 'Shake It Off'
23. 'We Are Never Ever Getting Back Together' and 'Chloe or Sam or Sophia or Marcus'
24. Hendersonville
25. 'dimples', 'accent'
26. 'Perfect' (co-written by Harry Styles and Louis Tomlinson)
27. A
28. 'Clara Bow'
29. 'sprinkler splashes', 'fireplace ashes', 'see you there'
30. Nils Sjöberg
31. A Chevy
32. Harry Styles
33. 'Castles Crumbling', 'Foolish One', 'Electric Touch', 'Timeless', 'When Emma Falls in Love', 'I Can See You'
34. Summer
35. 'All Too Well' and 'Mr Perfectly Fine'
36. Formula 1 United States Grand Prix
37. 2010 in *Valentine's Day*
38. 'Death By A Thousand Cuts'
39. Three: 'Shake It Off', 'Blank Space' and 'Bad Blood'
40. 'lost boys'

DECODE THE FRIENDSHIP BRACELETS

1. I Bet You Think About Me
2. Look What You Made Me Do
3. All You Had To Do Was Stay

LEVEL 9

1. 'I Bet You Think About Me'
2. Bombalurina
3. 'a secret', 'an oath'
4. Atelier Versace
5. 15
6. 2008
7. B
8. 'young', 'art'
9. *A Tale of Two Cities*
10. FALSE - Marjorie was an opera singer
11. Watch Hill
12. B
13. 'I Can See You'
14. Boys Like Girls
15. 'the 1', '22', 'Fifteen', 'The Lucky One', 'Two Is Better Than One'
16. 'Paper Doll'
17. The humidity had returned her hair to its factory settings.
18. 'You're On Your Own, Kid'
19. Three
20. A
21. Sarah and Hannah
22. The Chelsea Hotel
23. Snow White and the Seven Dwarves
24. Exactly nine years
25. 'Babe', 'Forever Winter', 'Run', 'I Bet You Think About Me', 'The Very First Night', 'Better Man', 'Nothing New', 'Message in a Bottle', 'All Too Well (10 Minute Version)'
26. 'kill', 'killed'
27. A couple who lived next door to her when she was a kid.
28. 'Sympathy is a Knife'
29. Wonderstruck Enchanted
30. 'I Knew You Were Trouble'
31. 'Soon You'll Get Better'
32. The Starlights
33. 'The Moment I Knew'
34. 'bad', 'mad', 'wise'
35. 'the grudge'
36. 'rich folks', 'wanna hear'
37. 'New Romantics'
38. Target
39. *CSI*
40. A

EXES

C	A	C	L	D	O	J	Z	R	A	T	C	J	H	Q
A	M	O	U	B	M	A	G	V	Z	A	H	O	A	D
L	A	N	C	N	I	K	B	Q	R	Y	G	E	R	T
V	T	O	P	O	X	E	W	J	T	L	B	J	R	R
I	T	R	O	T	R	G	L	X	L	O	D	O	Y	A
N	Y	K	Y	L	J	Y	T	C	J	R	F	N	S	V
H	H	E	S	U	O	L	M	X	O	L	I	A	T	I
A	E	N	Z	C	E	L	Z	O	H	A	O	S	Y	S
R	A	N	T	A	A	E	G	N	N	U	J	B	L	K
R	L	E	O	S	L	N	D	P	M	T	L	K	E	E
I	Y	D	B	T	W	H	B	C	A	N	E	K	S	L
S	K	Y	D	I	Y	A	X	S	Y	E	D	I	K	C
D	T	E	A	L	N	A	I	Z	E	R	G	N	T	E
A	K	U	P	L	P	L	L	O	R	Y	R	C	M	H
T	O	M	H	I	D	D	L	E	S	T	O	N	R	C

LEVEL 10

1. 'headlights', 'knife'
2. TRUE
3. 'I fell from the pedestal, right down the rabbit hole'
4. 'The Albatross'
5. C
6. 'ever changing'
7. Rascal Flatts
8. A
9. 16
10. 2010
11. 'penthouse'
12. A VMA
13. *Friends*
14. 'black dress'
15. FALSE
16. 'set fire to all my clothes'
17. Pat Monahan of Sugarland
18. Green
19. 'show up', 'bass beat rattling'
20. 'You're On Your Own, Kid'
21. 'I Can Do It With a Broken Heart' and 'Snow On The Beach'
22. 'the best', 'the same moon'
23. 'Swish Swish'
24. 'brought you in'
25. 'You Are In Love'
26. A
27. Audrey
28. 'Love Story'
29. 'Honey, I rose up from the dead'
30. 'Crazier' and 'You'll Always Find Your Way Back Home'
31. 'Old Habits Die Screaming'
32. 'State Of Grace'
33. 'you were too polite to do it'
34. Her spite and her tears and her beers and her candles
35. 'blink', 'crinkling'
36. Tom Hiddleston
37. Pop Bible
38. 'champagne problems', *evermore*
39. B
40. TRUE

DECODE THE FRIENDSHIP BRACELETS

1. The Smallest Man Who Ever Lived
2. Call It What You Want
3. This is Why We Can't Have Nice Things

LEVEL 11

1. A
2. 'romantic', 'safe', 'stranded'
3. 'The Bolter'
4. Ethan Hawke and Josh Charles – they starred in the film *Dead Poets Society*
5. B
6. Season 2 finale, Cece and Shivrang's wedding day
7. 'Cards', 'fools', 'fable'
8. A
9. 17 March 2023
10. The sequinned blazer Taylor wears for 'The Man'
11. 'Angels', Wembley
12. 'the glow of the vending machine'
13. metal
14. B
15. Leo
16. 'awkward blind dates later'
17. 'Summer of '69'
18. 'fancy stuff'
19. Idris Elba
20. *One Chance*
21. 'I Saw Her Standing There'
22. 'Begin Again'
23. 'begging for footnotes'
24. Emily Dickinson
25. 'he keeps his word'
26. Ethel and Bobby Kennedy
27. *Alice's Adventures in Wonderland*
28. Jack Antonoff, Taylor's longtime music collaborator
29. 'dagger', 'sharpen'
30. Lilac
31. A sound she hadn't heard before
32. 'Mom, I Am a Rich Man'
33. 'Beautiful Ghosts'
34. *Speak Now World Tour – Live*
35. B
36. At the 2015 MTV Video Music Awards
37. 'That's When', 'Bye Bye Baby', 'We Were Happy', 'You All Over Me', 'Mr Perfectly Fine', 'Don't You'
38. 'Forever Winter'
39. Tim McGraw and Keith Urban
40. 'The Black Dog'

COLLABORATORS

K Q Q T K I J D T P F Y E Y N L P H S F E U H V T
E G F R E H C J N V H N K Z H K E I T H U R B A N
O T Y H T D W H F X W H X Z M D Y E T S Y I S J I
K J N T A W O S L E S D M A R E N M O R R I S O X
C F J X R Y J O H N M A Y E R C A W E I X E A I C
E T R B L Q L Y A U C E S T I M M C G R A W T E H
F L O R E N C E A N D T H E M A C H I N E F H X L
E B L M L E U P Y T G X O B Q R Y B T F J V E T K
D U E K M J P L Z W T C L G O B G G H I Z N C F E
S U A A D P Q Z Q A I F H A X B V I P P Y Q H A N
H I W W K G F R X B Y L O R N R B F V D M K I L D
E C I F B W I P B N J N L T I A V B U P R A C L R
E O Z I B U E A I C P J B I H S D R F T A T K O I
R L O C W B C Q N T V R V Z A E S E Q T U B S U C
A B N W B R S T Z Q L V G Z Q M N T L C U R T T K
N I P H O E B E B R I D G E R S S A A R Q R E B L
A E F I N N X X N H S E O V S E K M T P E B N O A
J C H B I D K S H A W N M E N D E S X I L Y I Y M
M A D T V O X T J R Y A N T E D D E R U O E R S A
S I G M E N G S O A I G B T G C X V R E S N T O R
U L F P R U P P E H K B F O R I B J E B N M A Q X
A L H W X R T E J A J Q G L Q L R L L M O B T I N
M A A V X I Z D S G A R Y L I G H T B O D Y N R A
L T I I H E A Q D D F I S C Y D Q Y E V G D K O R
B J M K S X W E G P O S T M A L O N E N O K G N J

LEVEL 12

1. *The Rime of the Ancient Mariner* by Samuel Taylor Coleridge
2. Ronnie Cremer
3. Joey King, Taylor Lautner, Presley Cash
4. 'You're Not Sorry'
5. 'long hair slicked back'
6. 'ivy'
7. 'clowns', 'crown', 'beat'
8. A
9. 'bronze', 'spray-tanned'
10. A
11. CL moc lug loafer
12. 152
13. 'unglued'
14. 'Pumped Up Kicks' by Foster The People
15. *A Girl Named Girl*
16. 'You & Me'
17. 'That's the kind of heartbreak'
18. '(I Can't Get No) Satisfaction'
19. Glendale, Arizona, United States
20. 'marry', 'kiss' 'kill'
21. Kyle Newman
22. Kitty Committees
23. The Agency
24. 'I'm not afraid'
25. LeAnn Rimes
26. 'And I feel like my castle's'
27. Sea urchins
28. A paper plane necklace
29. Kellie Pickler
30. 19 April 2024
31. 'That wasn't the one I wanted.'
32. 'I Look in People's Windows'
33. 'Mine'
34. A stockbroker
35. 'blame, drunk on this pain', 'good years'
36. *The Road Not Taken*
37. William Bowery
38. Laura Dern
39. 'I had the time of my life fighting dragons with you'
40. *Fearless, 1989, folklore, Midnights*

DECODE THE FRIENDSHIP BRACELETS

1. Drinking Beer Out of Plastic Cups
2. 'tis the damn season
3. I Can Do It With a Broken Heart

LEVEL 13

1. A
2. FALSE – the books were written by Nancy Mitford
3. 'Big Deal' by LeAnn Rimes
4. 'held the door', 'mine', 'yours'
5. 'White Horse'
6. Nathan Chapman
7. *Taylor Swift*
8. 'coward', 'lion'
9. Toni Matičevski
10. A
11. Five: *Valentine's Day, The Lorax, The Giver, Cats, Amsterdam*
12. Felicia Miller
13. A
14. 54
15. 5 May 2015
16. 'revolution'
17. Joseph Cassell Falconer
18. 'Kiss Me' by Sixpence None The Richer
19. Lorrie Turk
20. Marjorie Moehlenkamp Finlay
21. 'esoteric joke'
22. Teffy
23. A
24. *Monster in My Closet*
25. TRUE
26. 'Breathless'
27. William Wordsworth, Samuel Taylor Coleridge, Robert Southey
28. 'fake it', 'make it', 'I did'
29. The Tangled
30. 12
31. Tuesday
32. Wednesday
33. 'Cold As You', 'White Horse', 'Dear John', 'All Too Well', 'All You Had To Do Was Stay', 'Delicate', 'The Archer', 'my tears ricochet', 'tolerate it', 'You're On Your Own, Kid', 'So Long, London'
34. *Lover, Fearless, Red, Speak Now, reputation, folkmore/evermore, 1989, THE TORTURED POETS DEPARTMENT, Midnights*
35. Humpty Dumpty
36. 'Snow On The Beach'
37. 'Better Man'
38. 'on a promising grown man?'
39. 'Cassandra'
40. A

T-FOR-TAYLOR SONGS

HOW DID IT END?

LEVEL 1 –	/40
LEVEL 2 –	/40
LEVEL 3 –	/40
LEVEL 4 –	/40
LEVEL 5 –	/40
LEVEL 6 –	/40
LEVEL 7 –	/40
LEVEL 8 –	/40
LEVEL 9 –	/40
LEVEL 10 –	/40
LEVEL 11 –	/40
LEVEL 12 –	/40
LEVEL 13 –	/40
TOTAL –	**/520**

So, do you **KNOW** Taylor Swift as well as you **THOUGHT** you did?